A Penny Always Has Two Sides

Steffie Steinke

PORTLAND • OREGON
INKWATERPRESS.COM

Cover : Steffie, 1949 (top); Steffie's foster mother, 1965 (bottom left); Steffie's mother, 1945 (bottom right).

www.inkwaterpress.com

ISBN-13 978-1-59299-481-6
ISBN-10 1-59299-481-4

Publisher: Inkwater Press

Printed in the U.S.A.
All paper is acid free and meets all ANSI standards for archival quality paper.

1 3 5 7 9 10 8 6 4 2

Contents

Acknowledgment

AFTER I HAD SOME THOUGHTS OF WRITING ABOUT MY CHILD-hood, maybe just for my children, I had no idea that the story would become of interest to other people.

I talked to Ingrid Vandermarel, a good neighbour and friend about it, and I was amazed how excited she became and how much she was willing to help.

And thanks to her help and never-ending encouragement, this book came together.

So Ingrid, I am so thankful to you that you never refused when I sent another ten pages to you and you carried on, helping with the editing and suggestions. I'll never know how I would have done it without you.

I would also like to express my gratitude to other people, known or unknown to me, who gave their honest opinion and words of enthusiasm, which helped so much too, to carry on and rewrite and correct and rewrite again.

For me the book became a healing process and I hope that, with my story, I can reach a wider audience who is interested in reading about my experiences.

With this book I have completely forgiven, but I have learned that it is so very hard to forget.

Foreword

THIS BOOK IS WRITTEN IN MEMORY OF MY BELOVED FOSTER mother, and of my mother.

It is a collection of my memories, which go back to my very early childhood, World War II, and the time after the war.

Many people my age will find some similarities in what we, as children, had to go through during and after the war. And of course later, growing up, we were able to realize the agony our parents or the people who cared for us were compelled to endure. They themselves were without means; they had nothing and yet they were the ones who carried us until we were able to live a normal life again, a life without fear and hunger. I must say, I still admire them, and the older I get, the more I wonder how they did it.

Depending on how memories come back to us or how they are remembered, they can be true or exaggerated or even fictional. Some memories are good and we love going back to the past to re-live them, while others are bad and haunt us forever. Some are a combination of true facts and recounted tales.

My memories, many of which are deeply anchored,

begin when I was almost four years old. They are still strong and often dominate my thinking and conscience. However, I am sure that they are mixed with some tales. I guess children remember things differently than adults and so forgive me if some names, locations, distances, or even facts are wrong. This is how I remember my childhood and my time as a young adult. And when I look back now, I realize that, in principle, these memories and the time I had with my foster mother, who gave me everything a child needs to grow up, namely love and security, made me the person I am today.

I experienced love and hurt and finally true happiness, and by writing this book, I hope I will be able to forgive, and maybe even to forget some memories. My foster mother always told me, forgiveness is the goodness of our soul.

EVERY PENNY HAS TWO SIDES

Things never changed until the very end—my mother was admitted to the hospital

As I SAT BESIDE MY MOTHER'S HOSPITAL BED, HOLDING HER hand, trying again to be close to her, I couldn't help thinking about my foster mother and asking myself why I hadn't been with her when she needed me, when she was at the end of her life.

On February 3, 2000, my half-brother Martin called to tell me that our mother was very sick and was hospitalized again. He told me that it didn't look good this time; it seemed to him that our mother was giving up. Apparently she didn't even object to being told that a hospital was better for her than staying at home. He said, "Before this, she was totally against going to a hospital but not this time. She agreed without any argument. And another thing: she doesn't eat anymore. Steffie, I tell you, she looks tired and simply wants to give up."

My mother had seen many hospitals in her time but in the recent past hospitals had been out of the question; she was afraid that she would not return home again. So maybe it was bad this time? I asked him if he wanted me to come but he said, "That's up to you. I just wanted to let you know what happened with our mother and if you decide to come, phone me. I will pick you up at the airport." And with this he hung up.

Of course I was shocked and my first thought was that I should fly to Berlin at once. So many things lay between us and we should make peace before anything happened.

I should have done it a long time ago. However, my second thought was, should I? Could I? Could I ever forgive and forget? Forgive, yes, I had done it in one way or another already; after all she was eighty-five now and time heals. But forget? I didn't know. I needed reassurance to fly to Berlin to see her. How could I talk to her now when she was so sick? I knew I had to make a decision quickly but I needed to talk to my family first.

Needless to say, everyone suggested that I should see her. Dietmar, my husband, said, "Fly and see her before it is too late." When I talked to my daughter, Sabrina, about it, she too suggested that I should not hesitate. "Maybe you will regret it later. I think it is better to see her now when Oma Rosi is still alive rather than go to her funeral." And my son said, "What a question, Mother, go, don't wait."

The thing is, except for Dietmar, the family did not really know what my life with her was all about. However, I did decide to go.

My son-in-law gave me his air miles and booked a flight for me and I phoned Dietmar's sister Ingrid and asked her if I could stay with her. She was delighted, saying, "Of course you can stay with me. What a question, Steffie, you know you are always welcome here. I'll be delighted to see you but it is so sad that your mother is sick. I hope you'll still see her and that she'll get better again. Just come soon. I'll be waiting."

So, two days after I had received the call from Martin, I called him back to say that I would come. I packed a few things and flew from Toronto to Berlin, Germany.

The flight was not a good one; we had a lot of turbulence and I felt lost and lonely. I constantly had tears in my eyes. But I made it anyway and was glad when we finally landed in Berlin.

Martin picked me up at Tegel Airport and after we embraced, he updated me on how my mother was doing. We then drove straight to the hospital.

When I saw her, I couldn't believe how much she had changed. She looked so frail and small, not like my mother at all. I had to hold my tears back again. She was sleeping and we didn't want to wake her, so we went for a little walk down the hall.

Like all hospitals, everything was clean but seemed so gray and, to me, looked hopeless, almost not real. Most doors were open and nurses were busy, some smiling, talking with patients in soft, soothing voices, others very grim, all work, no time for anything but their duty. I felt cold and tired from the flight and, as always, I felt unwanted when I was near my mother. Oh, how I hated hospitals!

She was awake when we returned and she looked at me in disbelief but smiled. However, when she looked over at my brother, who stood behind me, her smile was bright, mixed with love and affection. Was I jealous? No, I was not. How could I be; after all, she never gave me love before, so why should she now? As always, I felt uncomfortable when I was with her but I bent down to give her a kiss, and greeted her. I asked her how she was and if she was in pain but she hardly replied to me. She turned to my brother and asked him why I had come and said to him, "I must be dying. Is that why she is here?"

"Of course not," my brother answered. "Steffie came to visit you and not because she thinks you are dying, which you are not, right?"

My brother and I were embarrassed. We certainly didn't know how to handle this situation and my brother whispered, "She doesn't really know what she is talking about so don't be offended. Try to understand."

I tried. After a while he told me that he had to go back to work but that he would pick me up in two or three hours. I had the feeling that he wanted to escape from an ugly situation. I pulled a chair close to the bed and told him not to forget me or he would find me in mother's bed as well. He just laughed and left.

After a while my mother started to talk a little and became more alert. She even asked me how my flight was and introduced me to the nurse who came in with lunch. My mother told her that I had come all the way from Canada and with a smile, she said again, "I must be dying soon because why would she come and see me; it is not my birthday or Christmas." We all laughed and just took it as a joke.

The nurse turned to me and asked if I was coming again tomorrow. I told her that I would be staying a week and planned to see her every day. She nodded and mentioned that my mother wasn't eating. She said, "Maybe you would have more luck with her. She must eat or at least drink."

I looked at my mother and nodded. "I will try." She

left after placing the tray in front of my mother but just before she went out of the room, she turned to me and wished me good luck with putting some food into her.

The food was typical hospital food, nothing inviting, but probably good for her if she would eat it. I tried to feed her but she hardly opened her mouth. I now understood what the nurse was trying to tell me. I told my mother that she must eat, even if it was only a little, but she shook her head, saying, "I am not hungry!"

I tried a few times and made it clear to her how important it was that she eat. I said again, "Mother, if you don't eat, you will not get better."

She looked at me and answered, "I don't really care, but maybe I will try to eat later or when you come back tomorrow."

I was upset. "Tomorrow isn't good enough, Mother. At least drink a few sips." But she turned her face away and said, "Tomorrow!"

I had the feeling that she just wanted me to go away and stop pestering her and that that was why she promised to eat tomorrow. I looked at her again and thought to myself, she is so weak, maybe they should put her on intravenous. The nurse came back to check if she could take the tray back and was disappointed that most of it was still untouched. She took the tray and said, "So she didn't eat for you either. You know, we can't force her. She should eat but what can we do? I really hoped that you could get some food into her."

I answered, somehow feeling guilty, "I tried and I will try again tomorrow but don't you think she should be on intravenous?"

The nurse shook her head, "You should talk to the

doctor about that. This is not up to the nurses and the doctor didn't order it yet, so I can't do anything about it. Mention it to the doctor tomorrow. She will be in between 1:00 and 2:00 in the afternoon."

Mother fell asleep again and shortly afterwards my brother came to pick me up. We didn't wake her; we just left.

We walked to his car and he was all bubbly and wanted to talk but I was so tired, I just wanted to sleep. After all, it was almost six o'clock in the evening by now and I had been up for more than twenty hours. I told him that I was so very tired and that I didn't feel like talking. He understood. He drove me to my sister-in-law's without much conversation and I was certainly thankful for that.

When we arrived at Ingrid's house and she opened the door, she just took me in her arms and I felt warm and welcome. She asked us in but after telling me that he would pick me up tomorrow by noon, my brother took off.

Ingrid made some tea and a few sandwiches for us and we started talking. We are such good friends and even though I was tired, by now probably over-tired, we talked until very late at night. However, when we finally went to bed, sleep would not come for me for a long time and when my eyes finally closed, it was time to get up again.

The following days were almost all the same: mother did not eat and became weaker by the hour while I sat by her bed and watched her, feeling sorry for both her and myself.

Almost every day my brother would drive me to the hospital around noon and pick me up again around 7:00

p.m. Once or twice Ingrid drove but in general Martin looked after the rides.

My talk with the young female doctor was not very successful. I think she was not ready to give up on my mother yet and she told me that my mother should eat on her own. As she explained, "Your mother is still capable, but just a little stubborn. You must try harder to help her; she will probably start to eat again even if it is just for you. Her health is not bad enough to put her on intravenous yet and I think if we do, she will give up for sure. She is still alert and, as I said before, she should eat on her own." With that, she started to walk to the next bed.

Well, I thought, after all she should know. She is the doctor. Still, I did not agree with her because my mother didn't drink anymore either. My brother brought some food from a restaurant that night because we thought maybe she didn't like the hospital food. Yet again, she refused to eat.

During my visits, Mother would not talk much and when she did, it was mostly about money. She told me a few times that when she died, my half-brother would get her savings. After all, it was his father's money in the first place and of course it should now go to Martin. However, she said, "Even though you were not with me much, there will be a small sum for you."

I think she felt bad that my brother had received the bulk of her money. She must have given it to him before she went into the hospital, including the money for me, because every time Martin came, she asked him, "Did you bring Steffie's money?" For some reason, she insisted that he give it to me now. I was shocked by the constant commotion about the money. First of all, I hadn't expected anything, and second, it was embarrassing and reminded me of times I didn't want to remember. Worse yet, maybe she thought that this was the reason I had come to see her.

One day Martin did bring the bank book and gave it to me. I told him to stick it but he made me take it, saying, "That is Mother's wish and you take it. I wanted to give it to you later but you heard her, she insists. She wants you to have it now, so take it." When I took the book, I felt like crying. The whole situation was getting on my nerves and I regretted that I had come.

The amount in the savings account was small and, frankly, I was not surprised. So why the fuss? But again, as in the past, whenever she gave me something, she did it in a way that embarrassed me and whatever she gave me was usually not for nothing. She always wanted something in return; the hundred "thank-yous," the hugs and love and the affection which I couldn't give to her. However, this time I felt that she wanted something different, something more., Forgiveness, I assumed. I wasn't sure but when I told her to stop the talk about the money, because that was still all she had on her mind, she said, "But you must know that I love you too, not just your brother, and I think it is time that you not doubt this anymore."

I thought to myself, "Right, Mother," but I just told her, "Mother, don't worry about it; everything is all right."

I had forgiven her a long time ago and she didn't have to pay for it; that's how I felt about the money. I looked at her and told her that she should rest and that I believed her that she loved me as she loved my brother. She seemed happy about that and lay back and smiled.

What else could I have told her anyway? After all, I saw that she was slowly going into another world and would not stay with us much longer. I felt bad about my feelings but what could I do? It was simply not in me at this point to tell her the truth: that I never felt close to her, never felt that I belonged and that I would never forget—I simply couldn't, because regardless of what she gave me, it was never given with love but rather more as a duty. In other words, presents from her were meaningless and more an obligation for me. What I had missed was affection and love and now it all came a little too late. So I lied, and as long as it made her feel better, the lie served its purpose. I certainly did not want to hurt her. I prayed that God would forgive me for not loving my birth mother and also forgive her for having hurt me a lot during the time I was with her, actually until I got married.

Each day became harder to sit with her, trying to feed her, brushing her hair or cleaning her teeth. It was all so unreal for me, so false, and it made me sad too; I felt sorry for both of us since, after all, she was my mother. I was always so glad when Martin came to pick me up and I could go back to Ingrid's place. It felt almost like being rescued.

During the mornings, Ingrid made it very comfortable for me. We had a nice breakfast together and laughed a lot. Sometimes we went out at night, with my brother or without him; either way we had a good time. I was sad that my mother was dying, as I would be sad for anyone. Since the closeness was missing, my feelings for her didn't change. Unfortunately, we didn't have the talk I had hoped to have with her. I wished with all my heart that it would be different but there was no bond. I often thought it would make me so happy if I could love her but it just didn't happen. I realized then that it was simply too late.

I guess my brother felt differently. He must have been close to her, which surprised me since he had never shown love towards her or, as I had assumed, received much love from either her or his father. In any case, he was able to show an affection for her that I never had. I didn't feel anything for her other than sorrow.

My half-brother married young, as he explained to me once, to get out of the house. However, he later separated from his wife and after that he changed. By some means he became a different person, a cold and strange person. He never talked to me about his marriage or the reason why he left his wife. Actually he didn't talk about any-thing anymore, except his work. I didn't know if he had another woman in his life or even just dated one, and after a while I didn't ask him anymore.

By the way, my brother never divorced his wife. He lived in the basement and she lived upstairs in their house. When I asked him why, because I certainly couldn't have lived like that, he just said that it was better that way and certainly good for the children. At the time they sepa-rated, the children were in their teens, a boy and a girl; both were adopted and both were mentally challenged in some way.

Martin is a tall, good-looking man. We actually have a unique relationship in that I helped to bring him into this world and looked after him for a long time. Certainly, in the first two years of his life, I was more like a mother than a sister to him.

My brother's birth

His birth, like so many things in my life, was a shocking experience for me. I was just thirteen years old when he was born and I didn't live with my mother and her second husband, Willi.

On the day of my brother's birth, I was only visiting my mother because I had to every month. Due to a court order, I had to see her whether I wanted to or not and needless to say, I hated these forced visits.

It was a cold January day in 1949 and as always, I didn't want to see my mother that day. If I had known what I was getting into that afternoon, I wouldn't have gone. But it was month end and as always, my foster mother encouraged me to go and see my mother. She would say, "Steffchen, go and see her. After all, she is your mother."

Of course I knew that my mother was pregnant and that the baby was a little overdue, but the plan was that the baby be delivered in the hospital and frankly, when I knocked on the door, half frozen and hungry as always, I hoped that she would be in the hospital by now and I could go home again.

Instead, a strange woman answered the door and said,

"You must be Rosi's daughter, come on in. Rosi told me about you and you can help, since I need all the help I can get." She introduced herself as the midwife. She was called a little while ago to come because my mother wasn't going to make it to the hospital anymore. Apparently her water broke (whatever that meant) and her contractions were only half a minute apart. I was shocked to hear what was going on, didn't understand what the midwife was talking about, and was surprised by what I saw when I followed her into the bedroom.

My mother was lying in bed, perspiring and whimpering. After I said hello to everyone, I wanted to leave again because I felt very out of place. The midwife, however, stopped me at once and told me that I had to stay. She told me to go to the kitchen and boil water while at the same time telling my mother not to push yet and yelling over to my stepfather to hold on to the bed. Apparently my mother had polished the floor so well, the bed with the carpet was sliding all over the place. It was more like ice than wood and because space was limited, Uncle Willi, as I had to call my new stepfather, had the duty of stopping the bed from sliding to the outer wall of the bedroom.

The midwife had her hands full directing the whole situation but I had the impression that she had everything under control without my help. I desperately wanted to leave. Just being thirteen years old, I couldn't comprehend the commotion and I was just standing there, stunned and numb, not moving until the midwife told me again to go and boil the water, saying, "You must go now. It is important that we have that water. Boil at least two or more kettles, we need plenty." Then again, moving her hand towards the door and kind of yelling now, she said, "Goooo!" And then she was shooing me out.

I stopped objecting at once and went to the kitchen to look after the water. In a way I was actually thankful that I was able to get away from my mother and her wailing and the very forceful midwife. I got busy boiling the water but I couldn't stop overhearing the midwife telling Willi again to hold onto the bed and to calm my mother down, who by now was screaming, "I can't do this!" And to Willi, "I told you, you asshole, I didn't want this baby in the first place! You did this to me!" And again, "I didn't want this baby!"

Nobody was listening to her, of course, and over and over the midwife told her to concentrate on the delivery. "You must be brave," she said. "It will be over soon."

It was cold in the kitchen because the wood stove was not on and the gas stove didn't give off any warmth, so after the water was boiled, I went back to the bedroom to tell the midwife that the water was ready and that I must go home to my foster mother now.

My mother looked up and asked me not to leave. "Don't go yet, maybe you will still be needed here later. Please!"

The midwife agreed and told me to go back to the kitchen. "I will tell you when to come with the water." Since I couldn't go home, I gladly left the room again. However, the screaming became louder, in fact, at times so loud that I held my ears shut and thought my mother would surely die soon.

I heard the midwife telling her to hold onto my stepfather and that she would have another look. After a quiet moment, I heard the midwife say, "Rosi, you can push.

Push!" My mother was pushing and crying and then the midwife was yelling, "Steffie, Steffie, come! We need your help."

I ran in and was told to hold onto the bed, which was still moving all over the place. In order to stop it, I rolled up the carpet a little, like a stop, and tried to hold onto the bed with my foot and my arms, gripping with my hands anywhere that I could. I looked over at my stepfather for help because my mother was pushing hard but he had his hands full holding my mother down, so I had no other choice than to hold the stupid bed in place by myself.

In the meantime, the midwife told my mother in a normal voice to push again and a while later in a loud, almost screaming voice, "Push, push! Rosi, push, just push!" I looked over to Willi, who was a male nurse, but he was now absolutely good for nothing. He had fainted. The midwife saw it too; she shook her head and just said, "Men, where are they when you need them?" Then suddenly she cried out, "My heart, oh my heart!" and to me, "Steffie, you must take over. I will try to coach you but we need your help. I am not feeling well." She looked pale and as if she was having trouble with her breathing.

By now the midwife was holding her chest and sitting in a chair in front of my mother. So here I was. I didn't know what to do but the midwife told me to let my mother hold onto me and press my arm. "Try to hold the bed only with your foot." Again I looked over to my stepfather but he couldn't help because he was as white as chalk and still not quite conscious yet. And so I gave my arm to my mother and she held onto me and pushed so hard that we sailed right through the room with the bed and the carpet and whatever was in our way. The midwife somehow managed to stop us. My mother pushed again but suddenly the midwife told us in a very quiet voice that she could see the head and told me that I must do the rest because her chest pain was getting worse. Having just said that, she fell over. We learned later that she had had a mild heart attack.

Sweet. Here I was all on my own now, not knowing whom to help first, yet for some reason no longer scared. In a way, it was funny, at least I felt that this was a joke because they certainly could not expect too much help from me. However, when I looked around, there was no one else. When my mother cried out, "Steffie, the baby is coming, help me," I had no choice but to help her first. I stepped in front of her and when I saw the head, I, too, screamed, "Push!" and then I helped my brother come into the world, a bloody little package screaming at the top of his lungs.

It was January 31, 1949, and Berlin was suffering under the blockade. Not a pleasant time, but he was out to see the world anyway. He was a big baby and I was told later that he weighed thirteen pounds and looked like a three-month-old baby. Somehow Willi heard his son crying and recovered quickly. He kind of took over but my mother started to whimper a bit again and right away I said to her, "I will not deliver another one."

She laughed and said, "That is just the afterbirth." I, of course, again didn't know what she meant but Willi I hoped knew, and I was glad that he was able to help and take it from there, whatever it was. He told me to get the water and a pail from the kitchen and when I returned, he put the afterbirth, a clump of flesh and blood, into the pail. He then cleaned my mother, and I had to clean and sponge the baby and wrap him up. At first I was afraid to pick the baby up but after a minute or so I was almost perfect and my mother smiled and said, "Thank you, you did wonderfully," praise I was not used to hearing from her.

Since there was no telephone in the house, I had to go down to the nearest phone booth to call for help. The midwife was transferred by ambulance to a nearby hospital, where my mother was also admitted only three days later. My mother had, as she had experienced when she delivered me, a lung embolus again. Both the midwife and my mother were very sick but both came through the ordeal. As for me, I will never forget the birth of my half-brother. I thought for sure that I would never have children of my own, it had looked so painful to me, but then what did I know? I was only thirteen.

About four months later, having been home for just a few weeks, my mother was admitted to the hospital again. She had another embolus and this time they took me out of school for about two months to look after my baby half-brother. This created the bond I described earlier, a bond I miss a lot now. I think the main reason that we lost the closeness was because my husband, our little daughter, and I immigrated to Canada in December of 1961. Circumstances, time, and distance took away what we once had and that is sad, but I guess it was a natural process, something that couldn't be controlled.

Don't forget, she is your birth mother...

I HAD BEEN IN BERLIN THREE DAYS NOW AND MOTHER'S HEALTH
had not improved. I had hoped that before I had to go back
home, she would pull out of it and would get better. But no,
she didn't eat or drink anymore. I was frustrated and sad
because I saw that she would not recover before I had to go
home. The hope that we could put her into a home, which
my brother had managed to arrange for her, dwindled also.
I was sad about all of this but I faced the fact that I couldn't
change anything and so I prepared myself to say good-bye
in a few days without maybe ever seeing her again. I felt
awful, even if we were not close. She was after all my birth
mother and she was dying, and despite my strength, I felt
that something in me was dying also.

When I visited her on Wednesday, I actually had the
feeling that she was better. They had finally put her on
intravenous and I think that helped her. She talked, even
told me a joke, and her face had a rosy colour. Later, however, I realized that she was confused at times and nothing
that she said made sense. After an hour or so she looked
tired and soon fell asleep again.

Sitting beside her, I took her hand. We were not talking and the room was very quiet, when suddenly my mind started to play tricks on me. I was holding my darling foster mother's hands. I saw her and when I started to cry, she said, as she always used to say when I was sad, "Don't cry. I love you and never forget that." And after a pause, as if she was really in the room, she continued, saying, "Rosi is your birth mother and you did the right thing in coming here and sitting with her in her last hours." And in my mind I answered, "Yes, I know, but why didn't I come to you when you needed me? You gave me everything only a mother could have shared with her child, love and warmth, and yet I wasn't there for you when you needed comfort." She smiled at me, saying, "Don't worry, because you know I was there with you. I knew that you couldn't come. You didn't have the money for the flight. I knew it all!" I saw her face, that beautiful soft face with those warm eyes, and again she said, "Just don't worry! The main thing is that you loved me and I know that you always did. Give your mother comfort as long as you can. I know she regrets whatever she did to us, and remember what I told you so often before we had to part: forgive her, circumstances had a lot to do with our lives and as you know, a penny always has two sides. She, too, had to carry her lot. Forgive her."

A little while later, my mother woke up and told me that she had had a wonderful dream. Her face was relaxed and her cheeks were rosy. She smiled at me and whispered, "Forgive me." My brother came and after a moment I gave her a kiss and left.

I had to fly back early on Friday but Thursday, when I said my good-bye to her, I knew that she would not get out of the hospital anymore. She was sleeping again and did not wake up when I kissed her and told her that I had truly forgiven her, yet I couldn't forget. I whispered to her that I would write a book about our lives together and apart, and that maybe then, with God's help, my wounds would heal. And I, too, said, "Please forgive me, Mother, maybe it wasn't all your fault, since a penny always has two sides." Did she hear me? I will never know.

When I arrived in Toronto on Saturday, rather than on Friday, I was sad and tired and ever so glad that I was home again. I had had to stay overnight in Frankfurt because of bad weather and when Dietmar picked me up in Toronto and took me in his arms, I was so glad to be with him again. However, when he hugged me, he whispered that he had bad news. I knew my mother had died while I waited in Frankfurt for my return flight. She was gone forever. Apparently she never woke up after I left. I did not go back for her funeral.

Unwanted but not aborted

It was 1935. Hitler started to make more and more moves that let the world know that he was not as peace-minded as he wanted everybody to believe. That same year, my mother, Rosi Bezold, became pregnant with me. She was twenty-one years old and not married.

As I was told, at first my mother wanted to commit suicide when she found out what a situation she was in. She had nobody to go to, no one to talk to about it. Yes, she lived with her grandmother, Marie Scholz, but could she talk to her? Rosi was sure that she, of all people, would not understand her at all. Nobody would, not in 1935.

When Rosi was nineteen, her mother suddenly passed away after surgery, which was apparently successful, but an autopsy revealed that she had had an embolus in her lung and help had come too late for her. She was forty-two.

Two years earlier, her parents had divorced. After the divorce, Rosi's father, who owned a pub in Berlin-Neukoelln, had almost no contact with Rosi anymore. Despite that, he probably could have helped her. However, when she approached him and told him that she was pregnant, he just answered, "I have my own problems and you are old enough to support yourself. You got yourself into trouble, you can get yourself out of it again. Sorry, but you are on your own."

Rosi wanted an abortion but abortions were very dangerous and if discovered, punishable by jail. Either way, in 1935 it was a matter of shame to be in the predicament she was in. Her grandmother warned her not to have an abortion and so she opted to have the baby rather than end up in jail, or worse, die.

Mama, as she called her grandmother, was a very proud woman, well known from the years when she and her husband owned one of the best vegetable stores in Berlin-Neukoelln. She was also well known for playing *skat*, a German card game that she never refused to play when asked to join a group, even of mostly men.

Mama and her husband lost their fortune during the big depression. Shortly after the loss of the business, she lost her husband and later, her only daughter. So, the only close person she had left was her granddaughter. Poor now, but still proud and very proper, she could not allow this abortion. The shame brought on Rosi by having this baby would be awful enough, but to have an abortion was unthinkable.

The two of them lived in Mama's little cottage, which she had had before bad times hit Germany. The cottage was situated on the outskirts of Neukoelln and people like my great-grandmother, who had these little places that were cheaper than their apartments, moved out to live in them because they could no longer afford other living quarters. Times were bad, Germany was still on its knees, and most people who lived in these cottages were without work. They got by because they were able to plant their own vegetables and fruit, and they kept chickens and rabbits. Many parcels were on a fifty-year lease, leased from the city of Berlin. The little cottages, and some were only shacks, were built by the occupants but were hardly fit for all seasons. Most of them were not winterized, and had no electricity or running water. And to make matters worse, they were located where the newly built S-Bahn (a city train) passed every fifteen minutes, together with the regular trains and freight trains. The noise was loud, piercing, and disturbing but people got used to it after a while and even got used to sleeping without hearing the trains. But now even in the summer, it was no longer an ideal location, and in the winter, it was depressing. However, nobody complained.

In a way it was understandable that my mother's grandmother had little or no sympathy for the pregnancy. However, she agreed to let Rosi stay with her, a hard decision since they had no means of bringing up a baby, but it was better than having an abortion. There was no space, no money, no food, and no hope. My mother had a little job working behind the lunch counter in a department store cafeteria but the income was meager; two could hardly survive on it and now there was the baby. The thought alone must have been awful for both of them.

My father, Norbert Kristian, was of no help whatsoever. Being an officer in Hitler's SS, married, a father of four small children with the fifth on the way (due four months before my mother would give birth to me), he could hardly admit that he had made a girl pregnant. I later learned that my mother had to sue him to get at least some support for me. It was a small amount but better than nothing. Anyway, times must have been terrible for my mother.

Conceived where? But born in a cottage

AFTER EIGHT HOURS OF LABOUR, I WAS BORN ON JANUARY 15, 1936, at twelve noon. My mother, with the help of a midwife, had delivered me at home because the shame of having a baby without being married was too much to go to a hospital. The delivery went smoothly and nobody foresaw any problems. However, Mama was useless with a baby and the midwife suggested they should get some help for a few days. So Mama went to a neighbour by the name of Meta Pech to ask if she could help until my mother was able to manage on her own.

Meta had had her own share of bad luck and misfortune. She was forty-eight at the time I was born, a very good-looking woman, tall, with a beautiful complexion, pitch black wavy hair, and soft big blue eyes. She was married now but had borne a boy and a girl out-of-wedlock herself. The father of the children was an English Navy Officer whom she had met after World War I in Danzig, where she worked as a housemaid for another officer and his family.

Danzig was a pulsing city with a large international

harbour. Since Meta came from a poor farming family and was the third out of twelve siblings, the big city was like a dream come true and when she met him at her employer's house, her world became perfect. They fell in love and he promised her marriage and a good life. He rented an apartment for them and shortly thereafter, she became pregnant. They had a baby girl and called her Elfriede. Not long after Elfriede was born, Meta discovered that she was pregnant again. This time it was a little boy named Karl, who, I think, became the child she favoured.

Her lover told her, "We will get married as soon as I get called back to England." She applied for her immigration papers and soon after the birth of their son, he was called to return to England. When he left her, it seemed they had everything properly arranged and that he would return to get her and the children within a month or so. However, he didn't return and she never saw or heard from him again. The letters she sent to the address he had given her came back with the note "address unknown." She tried to reach him through the British Embassy but they didn't help, nor did the people she had worked for. As she was told, she was just his mistress.

He had left her some money but when it ran out, she moved with her two babies to Berlin, where by now most of her siblings lived and where she later met and married Herman Pech.

She told me afterwards that there was no love between them, but they got married anyway, she out of desperation and Herman because he needed a mother for his daughter from his first marriage. I don't know whether he had work at first, but later he was without work and income, and the income Meta earned by working out of their home for a toy company was hardly enough to feed all of them. She always used to say that they just made it, how, I didn't know.

Meta became pregnant several times but always managed to miscarry, fortunately so, because Herman liked drinking and also had affairs with other women. Once when she miscarried again, she almost died, but after that she was no longer able to conceive.

And so the Pechs had no children together, even though Herman would have loved to have had a baby with Meta. Meta, on the other hand, was glad not to have any more children. Times were tough enough and Meta already had her hands full. She was certainly not happy at all.

Although Meta and Herman were neighbours of my great-grandmother, they were not close and hardly knew each other. However, because neighbours could count on one another when needed, when Mama called for help, Meta didn't hesitate to come and see what she could do for them. Apparently that was the way she was, to be there for anyone who needed her. In principle she kept to herself but regardless of how busy she was, she would make time to help if she could.

Meta learned from Mama that the baby had arrived two days ago and that Rosi had to stay in bed and couldn't even diaper the baby. Meta asked her why she herself couldn't help her granddaughter but my great-grandmother just shook her head, saying that babies were not her thing. She was afraid that she would do something wrong and changing diapers was simply out of the question. Unfortunately, the midwife, who came for the first two days to help and was great, was called to another delivery and wasn't able to come any longer. So Rosi and

Mama were desperate and at their wits' end because the baby was constantly crying.

When Meta entered the cottage, she saw what Mama meant. Apparently I was screaming at the top of my lungs, not having been fed and needing to be changed. My mother was lying in bed and was crying, saying that she had no milk and was not yet allowed to get up to diaper me. "She tried," Mama apologized, "but it didn't work. She can't nurse, it hurts her and she is really too scared to even touch the baby."

Meta didn't understand and wondered to herself how a mother could be afraid to touch her own baby! So she just concentrated on me, saying, "First of all, we have to get the baby quiet and then I will have a look to see what I can do for you, Rosi." My mother fell back into the pillows and wept some more but Meta told her to be quiet because there was no need for crying and feeling sorry for herself. "I told you, first I have to tend to the baby and then I will see what I can do for you, so just calm down. When the baby is quiet, I will get to you."

Meta took me up and asked, "By the way, what is her name?" My mother answered, "Steffie, not Stefani, but Steffie, spelled STEFFIE."

"Ok, ok, I hear you. Steffie it is and I think it is a beautiful name. She looks sweet. Who is her father? Is he Jewish? She looks as if her father could be a Jew."

"No," my mother answered bluntly, "as a matter of fact, her father is an officer with the SS and he is married. He told me all that when it was too late. So now I have a baby I didn't want and I can't work. I have no hope and I don't know what to do. Maybe I will give her up for adoption. I don't know yet, I just don't know!"

Meta bent down to her and said, "Well, Rosi, look at her. She has such a cute little face and is sweet and pretty with her black hair and big eyes. Just love her. She needs love like all babies do. Just love her."

But my mother turned away and cried some more.

The first two days went well; Meta came to change my diapers and made sure I was nursing from my mother who, after all, did get the hang of it. However, she was still not getting out of bed because the midwife had told her to stay in bed for about a week.

On the fourth day, after Meta left and Mama had to go out for a while, my mother was alone with me and everything was fine until I apparently started crying and she got up to see if I was all right. I was told later that she took me up to hold me but couldn't find anything wrong with me, so she put me back into the bassinette they had made for me and went back to bed. Shortly after that she didn't feel too well and when Mama came home she told her that she was up for a short time because the baby was crying but now she felt sick and had a pain in her lungs and couldn't breathe. She also felt cold and had the shivers. Later that night she and I had to be rushed to the hospital, where Mama was informed that my mother was very sick.

She, like her mother, had a blood clot in her right lung and since she couldn't nurse, I couldn't stay with her and Mama had to take me back home. So Mama took me back to the cottage where she placed me into the bassinette but was otherwise useless again. She didn't even try and as she explained later, the baby was too much for her and she was too old for all of that. She called on Meta again and asked her to come but Meta told her that she was not able to come until the morning. "Give the baby a bottle and change her, she will be all right," she told Mama.

When Meta came the next morning to see how I was doing, she almost lost it. I was screaming again at the top of my lungs but Mama just sat there, doing nothing. Meta couldn't understand why my great-grandmother was not able to look after me, not even for one night, and she asked Mama when I had last been fed.

"I can't remember, but probably yesterday, still in the hospital, before I had to take her home. I don't know, the nurse didn't tell me and I forgot to ask. By the way, there is a note from the hospital telling us how to mix the formula." When Meta wanted to prepare the bottle, there was neither a bottle nor milk for the formula in the house. Mama explained, "I couldn't buy milk since I had no money and as for the bottle, I thought we had one but Rosi probably hoped to be able to nurse so she didn't bother to buy any bottles yet. And then, of course, I couldn't leave the baby alone, could I?"

"So the last time the baby was fed was in the hospital?" Meta asked her. "No wonder that child is screaming."

She took me up and realized that I was soaked as well, but she didn't say anything further because she was very frustrated. Then after a moment she looked at Mama and said, "You know what, I will take Steffie home with me. I can look after her all the time there and she will have what she needs. You are welcome to see her at any time and when Rosi comes home, she can take her back and hopefully by then she will be able to look after her properly." Mama was delighted and relieved, and agreed at once.

My foster parents

I LIVED WITH MY FOSTER PARENTS UNTIL I WAS ALMOST FOUR years old.

My mother pulled through but she stayed in the hospital for about three months and when people asked her how it all had happened, she explained that she became sick because she got out of bed too early after giving birth. She told them that she was alone and more or less said that if the baby hadn't cried then, she probably wouldn't have almost died and wouldn't have the open wounds on her legs now.

I had a happy life with my foster parents and whenever my mother visited me, which was very seldom, I was told that she was an aunt and that was what I called her. My mother didn't object. For me, my foster parents were my parents; I loved them and they loved me and so did everybody else in their family.

By the way, I never really met my great-grandmother; she died a year after she gave me to my foster mother. So everything I know about her is from stories, but I think she was a proud, honest person. She just didn't like babies.

Hitler provided...?

OF COURSE I DON'T REMEMBER MUCH ABOUT THE FIRST THREE years of my life, but my foster mother told me later that by the end of 1937, we moved from the cottage to a new apartment that was located in Berlin-Neukoelln. The apartment was part of a huge apartment complex where my foster parents got the job of superintendent. They apparently had to look after ten apartment buildings, each four stories high, part of twenty buildings in total. Herman looked after the park-like surroundings, the central heating, hot water supply and, in the winter, the snow removal, while Meta had to clean the buildings, which were finished with hardwood and carpeted floors.

The complex was built in a square and each corner was located on a different street. The whole area was modern, with a beautifully landscaped garden in the courtyard, a big separate conference building, and a large playground for children. It was one of Hitler's government's pride projects and not many people had the privilege of living there. Most tenants were government employees and high-ranking party members.

My foster parents shared the work of the complex with another couple and both parties must have worked hard. The apartments were very modern inside with built-in kitchens, full bathrooms, and central heating, very luxurious for the time, more or less like our condominiums now. The people paid a certain amount to the association before they moved in and also a monthly fee rather than rent, which was for the services provided by my foster parents and the other couple. It was the superintendent's responsibility to make sure that the tenants were comfortable and well looked after. The only difference that there was from today's condos was that the complex was not owned by the occupants but rather by the government. So it was modern and ahead of the times and thought of as a proud showcase of Hitler's generosity. Or so everybody said.

We had a fairly good-sized apartment on the main floor in one of the buildings, which was located at Woernitzweg Number 8. Like all the other apartments, it had luxuries such as central heating, warm and cold running water, and a bathroom with a tub. It must have been a big change from the cottage and I am sure my foster parents thought they now lived in heaven. And even though they did not have much time anymore, they gave me all the attention they could, in fact, I was told that I was actually spoiled rotten.

My foster parents had to work hard but they didn't mind a bit because now they were happy with their lives. My foster father had the little girl he had always wanted and my foster mother no longer had to worry about putting food on the table. Her husband did his part as well and it seemed as though both had a better marriage now.

I only vaguely remember my foster siblings. They too, loved and spoiled me; however, Karl, my foster brother, was drafted into Hitler's military soon after we moved into the apartment. He was still very young and I think he was Meta's favourite since she always talked about him. She told me later that he was a good person and that he loved me too, but as I mentioned, I don't remember.

After he was drafted, Karl came back for short holidays, but in 1943 he was reported missing. He never returned from the Eastern Front. My foster mother contacted the Red Cross and asked soldiers who had seen him and even fought beside him before he disappeared, but nobody could help her. She hoped for a long time to see him again, even after the war, but as with so many, he was gone and he never returned.

Elfriede, her daughter, was only with us a short time before she went back to Danzig. She never returned home. She was caught stealing and was in trouble with the law. Apparently my foster mother was very worried and sad about her but basically she was helpless and couldn't do anything. As far as I know, Meta heard from her once or twice after she left, but that was all. She didn't even know if her daughter was still alive.

My foster father's daughter Liselotte, or Lilo as we called her, was the youngest. We were only twelve years apart and I remember that she carried me wherever she could and helped my foster mother look after me.

I think we were a happy family. My foster parents worked hard, but at least they had work and food to put on the table, and I guess, as they saw it, the new government provided well for them.

My foster father joined the party; very faintly I remember that we had a big picture of Hitler hanging in our living room. I also remember that one day Herman was sitting high on a white horse and collecting money for the NSDAP, as they called Hitler's party. It was so exciting because my foster father took me up on the saddle and I was sitting right in front of him, riding with him on this beautiful horse.

So, I guess times were good for Germany. Nobody thought that Hitler could do wrong, or later, that he would lose the war he started. The main thing for everybody at the beginning of his reign was that he brought back law and order and I think people, especially the working class, believed in their leader because they had their dignity back, had work and new hope. And with all that, he blindfolded them, because they didn't see and didn't know his real plan or what he was capable of doing, nor the consequences they would have to pay one day for what he had done. They believed in him and what they were told, that Germany would be at the top of all nations and that nobody would ever be hungry again.

It must have been awful when, in the end, it all came to light. Hitler's ideas to overpower the world were evil. Nobody had the slightest idea of what it would do to everyone and how many lives it would cost, nor how it would end. Most Germans had no clue that he was murdering Jews and that he had no respect for life in principle. The Germans were under his spell; they trusted him. As I understand it, there were whispers and rumours, but nobody believed what they heard, simply because it was too awful and because it was known that if you opened your mouth and questioned what he was doing, you could be arrested or worse, killed.

By the way, according to the papers I was given when I turned twenty-one, my real father fell in Poland, in the second week of September 1939. He was one of the first ones to die in the first days of the war.

My mother gets married

I WAS TOLD THAT ONE DAY IN OCTOBER 1938, MY MOTHER came to visit us to tell Meta that she was getting married. His name was Richard Niemetscheck and my mother described him as a very good-looking man with pitch-black hair and a good build. He was a tool-and-die maker by trade and had a good job in a large company. She also told my foster parents that he had been married before but had no children. (My mother later learned that his first wife divorced him because he was an alcoholic and they couldn't have children.)

Anyway, Meta and Herman were glad for her because Richard seemed suitable and could provide her with what she needed, a home and hopefully love. My mother explained that I could continue to stay with my foster parents and that "Richard wants to have children of his own." This, of course, made my foster parents very happy because by now they loved me as if I were their own child and actually wanted to adopt me. However my mother didn't want it to go that far, saying she would consider it later, maybe after she had a child with Richard.

They got married in December 1938 and hardly ever visited us anymore. I don't think my foster parents missed her because I didn't like that "aunt" in the first place and my foster parents were sure my mother would stand by her word and let me stay with them.

My mother didn't show up again until the following summer and brought her husband, or my stepfather, with her. They had coffee with my foster parents and after a while I heard my mother arguing with them. They talked about taking me away from my foster parents. My mother wanted me to live with her and my stepfather. She even threatened that if my foster parents made trouble, she would go to court to get me. I didn't really know or under-stand what they meant but I knew it was not good and after they left, my foster mother was crying and took me in her arms and told me that they would never give me back to her. She said, "You are our little girl. Let them fight; we will fight right back."

Well, my mother went to court and I was taken away from my foster parents on December 21, 1939, three days before Christmas Eve. The state kept custody, so it was explained, for my protection until my stepfather could adopt me. So now I had a mother, a stepfather, and a guardian or social worker, and my mother, because my real father had been killed in the war, received the child care allowance until I was either adopted or turned twenty-one.

However, my stepfather never adopted me. Instead, through a court order, he gave me his last name "Niemets-check". It served two good purposes: first, it looked as if I were his legitimate child and I could say that he was my father not my stepfather without being ashamed of having a different surname than my parents, or worse, being called a bastard. And second, they would still receive the payments from the government, which wasn't much but better than nothing. When I look back now, I think it was probably a clever way of solving two problems with one decision. Certainly it was very much my mother's way, as I learned over time.

My foster parents were not even allowed to see me or come close to me anymore. So, in short, my life changed completely from one day to the next. I lost the most important thing, my parents, because that is what they were to me. My whole little secure world changed in just a few hours. The almost four years that my foster parents cared for me counted for nothing. That was over, finished. The court had ruled.

Three days before Christmas Eve 1939, when my foster mother packed my clothes into a little suitcase, my life changed forever. She gave me a big new doll and then she kissed me, holding back her tears, and told me that I must be brave and good. When I left with my foster father, I didn't know that I wouldn't see her again for many years and that I would only see my foster father two more short times in my life.

On our way to my new home, I started to become very scared and I cried; I didn't want to walk any further and wanted to go back home. I begged him to take me back. I even promised to be good because I thought I had been bad and that that was the reason why he was taking me away. But he just kept walking. (We could have taken the streetcar but I suppose he walked with me to stretch out our time together.) We came to an older part of Berlin where everything was strange and very unfamiliar. I started screaming and having a temper tantrum, but he didn't listen. Hiding his own tears, he kept on walking. We must have walked for at least an hour or so and I was so tired, but he didn't stop until we came to a street called Harzer Strasse. Here we entered an old apartment building. The big front hall was cold and felt hollow. We went through a small side door that led us into an ugly courtyard. We went into the next old building and up two flights of stairs. When we finally stopped and knocked on the left side door, I expected a monster to open the door but it was my "aunt".

The first days with my "new" parents

THEY OPENED THE DOOR, MY MOTHER AND BEHIND HER, MY stepfather, and asked us to come in but my foster father only hugged me and left me without saying a word. I just saw his tears and then he was gone.

My mother wanted to take me in her arms and give me a kiss but I pushed her away and started crying again. I wanted to have nothing to do with her. I didn't know it then but from the moment I stepped through that door, I was one step closer to being a very unhappy child for a long time.

My mother and stepfather lived in this old, typical Berliner apartment building with the front, back, and side buildings divided by a small dark courtyard. The buildings in the back hardly ever saw the sun because it was blocked by the front building. The courtyard between the three buildings served for the collection of the garbage of all three buildings and for the cleaning of carpets. The giant garbage containers were located against a high fence that divided our complex from the next property with almost the same setup. Not far from the garbage were two high posts with railings in between, and here people cleaned their carpets by hitting them with a big stick. The children used them as gym posts, etc.

Carpet cleaning was only permitted on Fridays until five and Saturdays until noon and, depending on the dirt coming out of the carpets, owners would be judged as being clean or dirty. Some people had really big carpets and were considered rich, and some had only small ones and were, of course, in the eyes of others, considered poor. However, in principle, almost all of the people living in this district were in the same boat and the talk about the neighbours was just gossip.

To me it was a very unfriendly area to look at and our windows pointed precisely in that direction. The neighbourhood was typically working class and people sometimes lived there until they died. The rent for the back and side buildings was cheaper and the courtyard was always cold and seemed unclean. As I learned later, the storage rooms or basement, where every tenant had a locker, was plain dirty, damp, and infested with rats, mice, and ugly critters. However, most people kept their coal and wood for the big tile ovens and kitchen stoves down there and in the winter they carried the coal and wood up again, in pails and baskets respectively. I was scared stiff when I later had to go down there with my mother to help her. The bathrooms in the side and back buildings had no tubs or sinks, just a toilet, and were not heated at all. In the winter it was so cold there that you would freeze your buns off if you didn't hurry up with your business.

My mother and stepfather had a very small apartment, just a bedroom and a kitchen. The bathroom, of course, with only a toilet, was dark, scary, and to me, always cold. And so was the entrance with the little hall, cold and dark.

Once my foster father had left, I had no choice but to step into the hall. I held onto my doll and wanted to hold onto my suitcase but my stepfather took it away from me and told me to follow them into the living room. We went to the combined living room/bedroom, which was furnished quite nicely but was dark even though it was still light outside. They had a Christmas tree standing between the two windows and when I saw it, I actually liked it very much; it was pretty. But when they asked me if I liked it, I said plain "no" because all I wanted was to go back home. My stepfather spoke softly with me and explained that I had to stay with them and he showed me the bed I was to sleep in. It was standing across from their big bed on one of the outer walls. As I looked at it, I thought that there was no way that I would sleep here with them, and so I asked for my little suitcase again, which my stepfather had in his hand now, but instead of giving it back, he told me that my mother would unpack it for me. He was actually very nice and in a way I liked him much better than my mother. He took me up and told me to call my mother "Mutti" (the German word for Mommy) and I should call him "Papa". Again I thought, I would never call them that, and I started screaming and wanted him to put me down. I didn't want him to touch me, even though he tried hard to comfort me and was talking in a soft tone to me. I am sure he understood my grief and confusion. He put me down and took my hand and showed me around.

It was getting dark by now so they lit up the Christmas tree, which they had put up early, just for me, my stepfather told me. (The German tradition was, and maybe still is, not to have a tree in the room until Christmas Eve.)

The tree was pretty. It had twelve candles and many beautiful bulbs and tinsel. For a moment I stopped crying. My mother wanted to take me in her arms again but I grabbed my stepfather, who took me up again and I put my arms tight around his neck as he whispered to my mother to wait a while. "Just let her get comfortable and maybe later she will come to you."

I saw that my mother was not pleased that I preferred my stepfather already, but she asked me with a smile if I was hungry. I shook my head. I didn't want to eat; I just wanted to go home to "my" Mutti and Papa. When she asked again, I answered with a clear "no" and screamed, "I want my Mutti!"

She looked at me as if she wanted to hit me but instead she went to the kitchen to prepare a meal. My stepfather followed her with me still hanging onto him. He was stroking my head and telling me that he knew that I felt strange. He spoke with his soft voice again and said, "I want you to understand that we are your parents now. The other father and mother were your foster parents."

I looked at him and asked, "Why, was I bad to my Mutti and Papa? Is that why they don't want me anymore?"

"No, of course not," he said, "but they never were your real mother and father. We are, so you should be happy that you are with us now."

I was so confused and I started to scream, "You are lying! I want to go home!"

Dinner was ready but I refused to eat, not even the dessert, which looked so good. All I wanted was to go home.

Later my mother told me that it was time to go to bed. My bed was a grown-up bed, with a big down feather duvet on top. I kind of liked it but I didn't want to sleep in it. However, my mother didn't give up and on top of that, even told me that before I went to sleep she had to get me ready and wanted to give me a sponge bath. I screamed, "I don't want you to touch me and undress me!" and then begged, "Please, I am not dirty. I had a bath in our bathtub this morning." Again my stepfather calmed me down but I continued to cry. I couldn't stop anymore.

My mother brought a big dish with warm water from the kitchen into the room, lifted me up on the table and started to undress me. I didn't let her touch me and she got really upset, saying to my stepfather, "Maybe we have made a mistake in getting her. I certainly cannot cope with all her fuss. I can feel that she hates me and it hurts; she should love me, after all, I am her mother." (I heard this line from her all of my life, actually in a way right until she died.)

My stepfather just said, "Give her time. She will calm down and hopefully soon she will forget Meta and Herman."

They put me to bed without being washed, without brushing my teeth, and without praying. My stepfather took me and just put me down, turned the light off, and left me in the dark. I hated the dark and I hated closed doors. (I still hate closed doors and completely dark rooms at night.)

At home, my Mutti always left the door open for me so that there was a little light coming into the room, but here they just closed the door and went into the kitchen.

I guess I cried myself to sleep and when I woke in the morning I started crying again. My mother was angry with me but my stepfather was still kind and patient. Yet I could feel that he was also upset, not because I cried but because he felt sorry for me.

Three days later, on Christmas Eve, I was so upset that I became sick. I ran a high fever and could not stop crying. They called the doctor and I think he told them that it wasn't smart to change my environment so drastically. He gave me some medicine to calm me down and before he left he came back to me and stroked my hair, saying, "All will be well, little one, and you will soon be fine."

I think my parents were not prepared to cope with a child who had been taken away from surroundings she loved so much. They didn't know what hit them but just hoped now that after a few days, I would calm down and slowly forget. Well, I didn't forget, not for weeks or even years. I was not the same child anymore; as a matter of fact I became shy but stubborn and very unhappy. It took so long to get over the change and apparently it was so bad that when my social worker visited to check with my mother on how we were doing, she was shocked when she saw me. My health was questionable and my weight loss was so visible that she asked my mother why she hadn't taken me to the doctor yet. My mother promised her to do her best and see the doctor at once. They all hoped that I would get over the separation from my foster parents soon.

On January 15th, they tried to celebrate my fourth birthday. I was not impressed and hardly looked at the really nice dollhouse they gave me. I wanted to go home. I missed my foster parents and my foster aunts and uncles more than ever. My mother and my stepfather tried so hard to make it a nice day for me but I did not even touch the cake and must have disappointed them very much. I think they hoped that I would at least like the dollhouse and would start to play again.

My stepfather had built the house and the furniture all by himself. It was very nice but I hated it. Later when I became more settled and started playing with it, I hit one little doll I couldn't stand so hard that it finally broke. I was punished for that by my mother. She told me that I was ungrateful but I didn't care.

Life goes on without my dear foster parents

Days turned into weeks and weeks into months and so time went by and I think I settled down one way or another after all. Or maybe I just gave up hope of ever seeing my foster parents again. I guess I started to blend in because I had no other choice.

I never got close to my mother. She was very strict and unforgiving, and I think the bond a mother has with her baby from the first day she holds it was simply never there. She had no understanding or consideration for a child. For instance, if she told me I should do something and I didn't do what I was told at once, I would get a slap right away. My foster parents had never hit me. She didn't see the need to explain or to show anything if she wanted me to do something. She just told me to do it and if I didn't, I was punished and was told that I was either stupid or lazy. And still, she wanted some affection from me. After the first time I pushed her away from me because I was so homesick and missed my foster parents so much, she didn't try to hug me for a long time afterwards. Later, of course, I became so afraid of her that I felt cold the moment she would come close to me. I tried, I tried so hard, but it just wouldn't work. We were miles apart and nothing could ever change that. There was no bond between us, not ever!

My mother was a good-looking person, not really pretty, but still attractive. Her hair was very dark and she had a nice figure but because my foster mother was so tall, I found her tiny and, anyway, I thought she was ugly, period. I also hated that she always had her left leg bandaged and that she constantly complained that she was in pain. It made me feel guilty because she told me so very often that it was my fault and that I would never be able to make up for what I did to her when she gave birth to me. "You know," she said, "it was after your birth that I became sick and now I have to suffer and have this big wound on my leg. Yes, it all started with your birth." Of course, I didn't understand what she was talking about but for the longest time she laid a guilt trip on me.

My stepfather Richard, whom I was calling Papa by now, was a kind person and the highlight of my day was when he returned from work and I could cuddle up in his arms. He was always there for me and played with me a lot. My mother became jealous and told him several times that he was spoiling me and that that was why I preferred him over her. The thing was, he made sure we had fun together. He made me laugh when he made faces and joked around. And he never hit me. My mother, on the other hand, never played with me, always told me not to break toys and not to touch things, etc., etc.

I still remember very clearly one time when she lost it because, while I was eating, I put my spoon too far into my mouth. She told me maybe twice to eat properly and after that, whenever I attempted to continue to eat, she slapped me because I still put the spoon too far into my mouth. We were on vacation and were eating in the hotel's dining room and after a while I started to cry because I didn't know how to put the spoon in my mouth anymore. Everybody started to look at us and I was so embarrassed but my mother wouldn't stop until my stepfather told her to quit and told me to stop crying by saying, "One day you will eat just fine. It is the spoon; it's too big for you. Don't worry, we will practice at home." I was not even five years old then. So yes, I was so scared of her and I told Papa once, when he suggested that I go to Mutti and give her a kiss, that I was not kissing her, that I hated her because she was a mean person. Both were shocked by my remark and at first nobody said a word. I, too, was upset about what had slipped out of my mouth and I ran to the kitchen and started to cry again. I heard them arguing but a little later Papa called me back and said to me, "What you just did was wrong and not nice, so go to your mother and apologize to her." After a pause, he continued, saying, "And give her a kiss because she is truly hurt and you must never say something like that again." So I went to my mother and told her that I was sorry, but I never gave her the kiss.

We had a piano, which my mother had inherited from her mother, and I think that music was her life. She played every day for hours and took piano lessons twice a week. I was allowed to come with her. Her teacher, Frau Bruening, was very strict too, but she allowed me to sit beside her when she gave my mother a lesson and she taught me how to knit. I really liked the piano teacher a lot. As a matter of fact, my mother was a different person when she played the piano and I liked that person much more. I loved to watch her play and could listen to the sound for hours. She played beautifully and I think this made me love Beethoven and Bach and many other classical composers.

She also took me out to go, as she called it, window shopping, and I remember these were fun times. We would go by streetcar to a well-known department store. We would start at the main floor and go by elevator up all the floors until we came to the café where we sometimes had a piece of cake, with coffee for my mother and hot chocolate for me. The toy department was on the fourth floor and, of course, was my favourite department. I was allowed to look at all the wonderful toys and sometimes Mutti would buy me something. Mind you, not much, and mostly colouring books which I didn't like because I didn't colour well enough for her and at times she screamed at me saying that I could do better. However, a few times she would buy me a little doll or a game. Once, I got a post office and Papa played with me and bought stamps from me. But my favourite toy was still the doll I had brought with me, my last present from my foster parents. I knew my mother didn't like that doll one bit, but I think she didn't have the nerve to take it away from me. She never told me to be careful not to break it either.

In the morning we had a routine: after my stepfather left for work, my mother would start the fire in our *Kachelofen* (tile oven) so that it would get warm in our room. After the room warmed up a bit, she would check if I was awake, so that she could get me up to wash and dress me. Sometimes I pretended that I was still sleeping because I was scared to start the day since I never knew what it would bring. Actually, it was neat to pretend that I was still asleep because I could follow my dreams to be somewhere else, playing with other children or laughing about my stepfather's jokes. However, eventually I had to get up, whether I wanted to or not, and the day would begin. After I was washed and dressed, she would clean the apartment completely. She was a clean freak and never missed a spot. Finally, after all of that was done and our little apartment was clean and spotless, we would eat breakfast. I hated that routine. When I was with my foster parents, I was a child; now I was treated like a grown up. I wished so much that I could play with other children again or could play without always being told not to break things or to do things I didn't like doing. Needless to say, it was always a struggle to face a new day. I still get the shivers when my memories go back to these mornings and I realize how unhappy I was with my new life.

The war at home

By NOW I HAD BEEN LIVING WITH MY MOTHER AND STEPFATHER for over a year. Life was full of restrictions and stresses that a child should not experience. My mother had a loose hand and she could strike at any time. My stepfather, however, was always kind, and I truly loved him. Unfortunately, I just saw him at night when he returned from work or on weekends. He played with me whenever he could or I was on his lap and he would read fairy tales to me, which I loved so much.

I soon realized that my mother was not too pleased by my constantly clinging to him. She always complained that I would never come to her, that I would rather stay away from her. At first my stepfather would tell her that she had to give it time, but later he told her outright that it was her own fault, since she showed no affection to me either and that she had to learn how to give love before she could expect it. And, he mumbled, maybe she was not even capable of loving in the first place. I didn't understand what he was talking about and I sure didn't ask, since I sensed that this was adult talk. They were fighting a lot lately and shouted at each other and it was so upsetting because I believed it was all because of me.

Also, lately, my stepfather came home very late and my mother said that he went to bars and was drinking again. He acted strange when he returned from "drinking" because he always talked funny. It made Mutti very angry when he talked like that but he didn't seem to care. He was sometimes outright mean to her and said bad things, but he never shouted at me. As a matter of fact, he always told me that I was the only sunshine in his life and he called me all sorts of sweet names, which I can't translate into English.

When he was sober again, he promised my mother that he would stop drinking, but he never did.

My mother later told me that he was an alcoholic before they were married but stopped drinking after they met and he had promised never to drink again. So much for that promise.

Wally, my mother's girlfriend

My mother had a girlfriend named Wally, who lived right below us. I learned later that Papa couldn't stand her so they only got together when Papa was at work. Mutti would knock on the floor with a broom stick. When Wally knocked against her ceiling once, my mother would go down. When Mutti knocked twice, Wally would answer with one knock and would come up to our place. It was kind of like a phone.

Wally was funny and I sort of liked her but when she came to our place, my mother often told me to go and stay in the kitchen because, as she said, my ears were too big to listen to what they were talking about. Or if Mutti went down to see Wally, she would leave me all by myself. She always promised to come right back, saying, "It is just for a moment, so be a good girl." But it always seemed like a long time to me and I was bored and didn't know what to do with myself.

One day my mother went down to see Wally and I felt bored again. I tried to do something "useful" (my mother told me often that I was useless) and so when I looked at the kitchen window, I thought it needed cleaning. I got a chair and climbed up and opened the window. With a cloth in my hand and a dish of water on the window sill, I started cleaning but I lost my balance a bit and almost fell the two flights down. However after a little struggle, I got a grip again and continued to clean.

A neighbour from across saw me and started to scream, "Get down, Steffie, get down!" But I pretended not to hear her. However, my mother must have heard her too because suddenly she was beside me and grabbed me. She held me tight in her arms and in a way I was glad she had come, but when she put me down, she hit me and hit me and wouldn't let up until Wally, who must have come with her, took me away from her. My mother cried out and said through her tears, "She could have been killed. She could have fallen and could have died. Richard would have killed me; he must never know that I left her alone. It was wrong. She is too young to be left alone." And again, "He would kill me if he hears about it." And then she looked at me and said, "You are so bad. I don't know what to do with you anymore." Wally looked at me and then said to my mother, "Rosi, you don't mean that. You are upset because you love her and you are in shock."

I don't think my mother ever told any of that to Papa.

I walked out

After that incident, I was not allowed to stay alone anymore, not even in our kitchen. Instead, I had to stay in our dark little hall. The kitchen door had a window so a little bit of light came through from it and made the hall just a bit brighter so that at least I wasn't sitting completely in the dark. I sat on the floor and heard them whispering and laughing and I waited until my mother would say that I could come back into the room. When she went down to visit Wally, I had to stay in Wally's little hall, which had the same setting as our apartment, it was just a floor down.

One day, Wally came up to visit and I was sent to the hall again. At first I was sitting there, bored and waiting for the magic word from my mother that I could come back into the room, when my eyes caught the entrance door. Not even hesitating, I opened it and walked out into the hall and ran down the two flights of stairs into the ugly courtyard, through the big hall of the front building and onto the street.

Oh, what a feeling! I saw children and watched them play and soon they asked me to join them and I had a ball.

We played for quite a while before my mother came

running toward me, pulling me by my arms and dragging me up to our apartment. I knew I was in big trouble and promised right away that I would never do that again. But it didn't help. I got a bad spanking and thought again, as I did so often, that this time I would die for sure before she would stop, but eventually she did and I was still alive.

After she was through with me, she told me to get my coat and she packed a little suitcase with some of my clothes. When I asked her why, because I hoped that I could go back to my foster parents, she said, "You were so bad this time that I will call the social worker, who will pick you up and put you in a reform school."

I wanted to know what a reform school was and she answered, "It is a school for children who are very, very bad. It is like a jail for bad kids." I certainly didn't want to go there and begged her not to call, but she left me for two hours in the hall, waiting to be picked up.

The waiting time was worse because whenever I heard somebody coming up the stairs, I thought they were coming. I was so scared that I shivered and finally threw up. My mother cleaned up the mess but still made me wait.

After a long, long time waiting, I had to go to the bathroom. My mother came out of the room again and told me that, if I promised never to do something like that again, she would call the social department back and cancel everything. I promised at once. I will never forget that incident. I had nightmares about it for a long, long time.

Again, she never mentioned any of this to my stepfather, who was coming home later and later. Most of the time he went drinking and then he would tiptoe into the room and sometimes behave very strangely and silly. My mother talked to Wally about it and said that he was drinking and that she thought he was having an affair as well. (I sure didn't know what that meant.) She continued to tell Wally that they hardly talked anymore and sometimes he was so drunk that he peed and wet his pants. I could tell that my mother was very unhappy about Papa's behaviour. Wally said several times, that if she were my mother, she would divorce him. (Again, I didn't know what she was talking about.)

Papa and my mother had many fights now. Often Mutti took me with her to look for him when he didn't come home or was late. She explained to me by saying, "Your father is sleeping around and drinks himself silly and I need proof that he has another woman." I didn't know what she meant because when he came home, he was still nice to me. I surely didn't know why she always either screamed at him or didn't talk to him at all. Sometimes, when they didn't talk, they just wrote notes to each other. And what did she mean by "sleeping around"? I had no clue but was afraid to ask her. However, I knew by now that "drinking" was a bad thing to do.

We would go from bar to bar and sometimes find him and sometimes not, but whatever happened, it was always embarrassing. The fights between them were frightening and at one time or another I thought for sure that Papa would kill Mutti, at least she screamed like I did when she hit me for doing something wrong.

Mutti cried a lot and stayed in bed often. She explained to me that she had thrombosis in her leg and that it hurt more and more. She wore the bandage regularly now and when she changed it, she made me look at her leg and the open sore. It looked awful and I really did not want to see it but she insisted that I look at it. After all, she would say again and again, "I have had these sores since you were born." I couldn't understand why she always blamed me because I had never hit her or banged her leg. I just didn't understand why it was my fault at all, but when she showed me her leg, I felt as I always did, guilty!

Papa came home drunk now almost every day and had this funny smile on his face. He still played with me, but Mutti didn't like it and would tell him not to touch me. However, he wouldn't listen to her and continued to make me laugh, played with me and my dollhouse, or drew pictures for me. I sure loved him. He was always good to me and so funny. The only thing I didn't like was the smell out of his mouth. Often he pointed to my mother and whispered if she was mean to me again because, he explained, she was mean to him, too, and we both giggled about it. It was our joke between the two of us. Mutti must never know that we both had the same problem with her.

ℬombs were falling
over ℬerlin

By now the war became much worse than people had expected. After Hitler marched into Austria and invaded Poland, the war had begun and there was nothing that could stop him from going further. He took Denmark and after a lot of resistance, Norway, and on May 10th, 1940, he marched over the borders to capture the Netherlands, Belgium, and Luxembourg. On June 14th, he was in Paris, France.

In August 1939 Germany and Russia had signed a non-aggression treaty, but following a deterioration of relations in 1940 and early 1941, Hitler conducted a massive attack on Russia in June of 1941, which started the fight against Russia.

Sometimes when my parents didn't fight and Papa was sober, he would read the newspaper to my mother and they would talk about these things but I didn't understand a word. Actually I didn't even know what war really meant until the planes flew over us and dropped bombs.

After Hitler made air attacks on the British, England bombed Berlin on August 26th, 1940. It was the first time, resulting in surprise and disbelief for the Germans because they were told that England would never be able to reach Berlin. Nevertheless, one day they were there and the Germans were surprised, upset, and disappointed, but they still believed in Hitler and saw him as the greatest warrior of all times. They were all blinded by the way he tried to conquer the world. Most people didn't know about the destruction, the Jews and their suffering, and his plan to destroy millions of them. If somebody doubted Hitler and was found out, he was either put into a camp or murdered, regardless of race or status and most of the time nobody knew where these people ended up. They just disappeared.

The soldiers fought in the name of the fatherland and, of course, were not allowed to express their opinion either. Hitler blindfolded almost everyone and the few who saw what was coming couldn't do much about it. I think my stepfather was one of those people who didn't believe in Hitler and his politics. I never heard him praise our "Fuehrer". I never heard him say "Heil Hitler" or saw him wearing a little button, the sign that he was a party member. Maybe that was his downfall at work. Mutti complained often that he did not get ahead because he hadn't joined the party. Obviously he was good at his work. He was needed and his company relied on him and maybe that was the reason why he was drinking: the pressure and stress of staying out of everything and yet still producing what was asked of him. I don't know; this is just my assumption. I still find excuses for him because at the time, he was the only person I had and trusted.

It was 1943 before somehow people realized what kind of man Hitler really was, but by then, of course, it was much too late. Nobody could open their mouth and say what they thought. Germany was under a complete dictatorship and I guess most people didn't even know how they had slipped into it. The whole country was like a big prison and everybody did what they were told to do. And so the masses screamed on, "Heil Hitler."

Papa was still at home, not like all the other men who had to fight and die for the "fatherland". My mother said he had a very important position and that was why he hadn't been drafted yet. However in contrast to other wives, she wasn't very happy about the fact. She said to Wally that it would do him good to serve, at least it would stop him from having affairs and maybe even from drinking.

I lost a ration card

I GUESS MY MOTHER'S LEG BECAME WORSE BY NOW BECAUSE SHE didn't go out much anymore. She even stopped going to her piano lessons.

I turned six and was to start school in September when one morning Mutti said to me that I was old enough to go shopping for her. She gave me a big shopping bag with a wallet inside, and told me that everything I needed was in the wallet: the money, the ration stamps, and a note for the sales clerk. She also said to me, "You mustn't lose anything, otherwise we will have nothing to eat. Just give the bag to the sales clerk. She knows you are coming; I talked to her yesterday." And again, "Be careful," she warned, "and after you are done with the shopping, come home right away."

I took the shopping bag and the empty milk can and promised to do what I was told but before I left, my mother called after me again that everything would be fine and that she had talked to the sales clerk yesterday. "Just be careful. Don't drop the milk or the shopping bag and make sure that the wallet is back in the bag. Don't play around and come straight up." And after a pause, "Just don't lose anything."

I think she was worried, and yet she sent me shopping expecting that I would do just fine. I felt proud and very important and grownup for being allowed to go shopping all by myself.

I jumped down the stairs and almost fell, but then went straight to the milk store. I did what I was told and when I came back Mutti took the shopping bag and looked for the wallet and found that everything was in order. I unpacked the butter and placed the little milk can on the table and she praised me and said that she was very proud of me.

From that day on I went shopping almost every day, not only to buy milk and butter, but also all the other groceries as well. I went to the baker to buy bread and buns and there I was sometimes allowed to get a piece of cake for myself. People would often say that I was too young to go shopping all by myself. They would make remarks like, "Isn't she a bit too young," or "The responsibility, it's much too much for a kid of her age." But I thought it was great. I liked going shopping. And for months everything went fine until one day when I went to the bakery. As always, I gave the shopping bag to the clerk and she looked for the wallet, but this time she couldn't find it. She asked me if I had the wallet but I shook my head and said no, it must be in the bag. We both looked again but there was no wallet. She handed the bag back to me and said, "Maybe your mother forgot to put it in?" I was sure, however, that my mother hadn't forgotten. I saw her putting it in before she gave me the shopping bag and so I looked again, but the wallet wasn't there. It must have fallen out or maybe it was stolen? I couldn't explain how I could have lost it because I had gone straight to the store.

I just didn't know how it could have happened. The worst thing was that I would have to tell my mother. I was so afraid, because I knew she wouldn't believe that I hadn't played around with other kids. She would be unforgiving. I knew that for sure.

Why did this happen? I stood there and didn't want to go home and started to cry. As a matter of fact, I was so afraid to go home that my crying became uncontrollable and caught the attention of other customers. I overheard one woman saying to another, "I saw it coming. I thought she was too young to go shopping by herself."

When the salesclerk overheard her remarks, she cut into the conversation saying, "As you know, this little girl always comes here. Her mother is sick so she has to help and you know what? She is doing a good job. I am sure the wallet will be found." The woman shut up by shaking her head and making a face, but I was grateful that the clerk had stood up for me and praised me, even if I had I lost the wallet.

A neighbour, who had just come into the store, saw me and asked the clerk what had happened and why was I crying and could she help. The clerk explained everything and the neighbour offered to take me home. She bent down to me and looked into my tear-filled eyes. "Maybe the wallet is still at home, *ja*? Or we will find it on our way back. But whatever will be, I am sure your mother will understand." She unfolded a clean handkerchief and wiped my face and asked me to blow my nose. She then took my hand and said again, "I am sure your mother will understand." Her voice was soothing and I believed her and hoped that she was right.

Well, my mother understood all right, because as

soon as the neighbour left and my mother closed the door behind her, she screamed at me and told me that she always knew that this would happen one day. "I can't trust you with anything," she said, "I should have known better." She took me by my shoulders and shook me back and forth, and continued, "I told you to go straight shopping, but you can't listen, can you? What did you do, did you walk or did you jump again? Or even play with other children? Answer me!" she screamed. But I just stood there not saying anything because she wouldn't believe me anyway. She let go of me and looked at me and then continued, still screaming, then talking, "You know what, young lady, you will have no bread, buns, or any goodies from the bakery for a whole week. That's all there is to it; I think this will teach you not to lose anything."

This of course meant not much for breakfast or lunch. No bread, buns, or goodies, period. Oh well, I thought, maybe I won't eat at all. I wondered if she would get worried. I should try it, but then maybe not, because she would probably get mad and would hit me again. So I stopped crying, and said, "I am sorry, it will not happen again," but my mother just answered, "It better never happen again."

Mother did the shopping by herself again. She took me with her, of course, but I hated it because she told everybody, whether they wanted to hear it or not, that I lost the wallet with the ration stamps. She said, "I am still sick and should stay in bed with my leg, but I can't trust Steffie any longer. I simply have no other choice than to walk all the way back and forth, down the stairs and up again to do the shopping myself. I can't rely on Steffie and there is nobody else who can help." Oh, it made me feel so bad that I wanted to hide.

Every time we passed the bakery she told me not to even look at the nice things they displayed in the window. "Remember, you can't have anything," she said over and over again. "You better never forget. Don't look, you just make it worse for yourself." She, however, bought bread, but as she explained, "This is for Papa and myself. You will get your portion next week again." And she continued, "That's what happens when you play around rather than pay attention to what you are told."

Everybody had ration cards for almost everything by now and I knew that without them we would not have much to eat. I understood all that perfectly, but since I liked buns and bread very much and I realized how bad it was to do without them, I wished she would have given me the spanking I usually got when I did something wrong. I really didn't understand the new punishment I got this time and I asked myself how she could be so unfair.

I wondered if my father knew that I had lost the ration stamps, but I didn't want to ask because I was afraid that this would make things worse for me, and since he didn't mention anything to me, I pretended that everything was fine and that I didn't want to eat bread.

By the way, a neighbour found the wallet with everything still in it and nothing missing. She gave it back to my mother but my mother didn't tell me about it until a week after my punishment was over. I must have lost the wallet when I jumped a few stairs rather than walking down slowly. I didn't know better, I was just six years old and when I was on my own I jumped down the stairs rather than walk. All I knew was that I would have preferred the spanking I probably deserved rather than have no bread or buns for a whole week. I started to hate her.

More bombs were falling over Berlin

BERLIN STARTED TO BE BOMBED MORE OFTEN AND WE WERE told to go down to the shelters whenever the sirens came on announcing that another air raid was expected. It was mostly during the night that the alarm, a terrible noise, would wail. My parents (if Papa was home) would take me out of bed and we would rush down to the shelter. Sometimes it was just for a short while but often we had to sit there for hours. But it was always scary and many children were crying. Often we could hear the planes flying right over our apartment buildings and the noise it made when the bombs came down. People knew when it was close to us and they would hold their breath or pray because they never knew on which building the bombs would fall. We all felt relieved when a different sound of siren would wail and the air raid was over. It was a good feeling to know that everything was still ok and that we were safe, this time anyway.

One time Papa was not at home when the alarm came on. As we were rushing down the stairs, I started to cough. I had the whooping cough and had a bad spell. As a matter of fact, it was so bad that we didn't make it down to the shelter. I couldn't stop coughing and started to throw up as well. Mutti held my head and told me that we would not go down because we had simply run out of time. My mother made sure that the curtains were closed tight and that no light was visible from the outside. Just moments later we heard the planes coming in, a frightening noise. It was terrible in that it was closer than ever before and it scared me so much that, for the first time, I hung onto my mother. She was surprisingly gentle and stroked my hair and said, "All will be well, don't worry. God will stay with us." It was the first time that she mentioned God and I didn't know whom she meant but for some reason I trusted her and the strange person "God" who, as Mutti explained, lived in heaven. And I then remembered that my foster parents used to pray with me to him.

The raid was a bad one. Bombs were falling everywhere and by now, we were both scared. We hung onto each other, but God stayed by us because when our building suddenly started to sway, we thought for sure that we had been hit and that we would die. But nothing happened to us, just a few windows shattered. It was amazing. However, when we later went down to see if everyone else was all right, we saw the damage and couldn't believe that we were alive and our building was still standing, almost undamaged.

Yes, our building was fine, but the building next to us was completely destroyed. It was hit by a bomb that went straight down and exploded from the inside out, miraculously leaving our building standing. Rescue people were already working, trying to get people out, mainly from the shelter. They had to make sure that the fire, which started because of the broken gas lines, was under control, and they listened for noises and knocking and looked for any movements under the rubble. But only a few people came out alive and many died that night, and I thought, "God truly stood by us." He had protected us and whoever he was, I started talking to him as I did when my foster parents prayed with me, thanking him for all good things and asking him to help me when I was in trouble. I started to trust him and I realized suddenly that I had a friend.

Much later my stepfather came home and when he saw what happened, he was surprised that our building was not damaged at all and that we were fine. He took me in his arms and gave me a hug and even kissed Mutti, which I seldom saw. He was truly upset about what happened and said to Mutti, "Maybe you and Steffie should move to the East. I heard that Hitler is evacuating mothers and children."

But my mother didn't want to hear what he had to say and became angry. She replied, "I take it, you want to get rid of us, so you can continue your affairs without us being around?"

He just looked at her and turned away from us. But then he came back and answered, "First of all, Steffie is here and I don't want to fight in front of her, but for your information, I'm not having an affair and I meant well when I said that you should get away for a while. Even if it is just for the child, because it will get worse before it gets any better."

My mother, however, just laughed and said, "Not a chance. We will stay."

"Fine," he told her, "suit yourself," and left.

My first school year

I STARTED SCHOOL IN SEPTEMBER 1942 AND I WAS EXCITED about going. However, right after the first few weeks or so I started to hate it because I didn't do anything well enough for my mother. At first my teacher was so pleased with me because I picked everything up well. As a matter of fact, at one point I was ahead of everybody, but as soon I came home, I was in trouble. My work was never the way my mother wanted to see it.

We had little blackboards and chalk at first and when I showed her my work, she made me write things over and over again. Later, when we had notebooks and she saw mistakes, she ripped the pages out and again, she made me do things over and over again until I was confused and didn't know what was right or wrong. Regardless of how much I tried, everything came out wrong anyway and often she would slap me. She tried to explain arithmetic to me but when I came to school and I applied her teaching, I made mistakes and got bad marks. I gave up on school fast and didn't even try anymore.

My teacher noticed the change and one day she asked, "Are you all right, Steffie, or is something wrong?" I looked at her in terror. I couldn't tell her that my mother hit me for every mistake I made. And if I would tell on her to my teacher and she would hear about it, she would do worse than just slap me, she would send me to reform school and I certainly didn't want to go there. So I just swallowed first and then told her that everything was fine. I knew that she didn't believe me and that I was lying to her, but I couldn't tell her anything, no way! Mutti would punish me for it and that would be worse than lying.

The teacher must have talked to my mother anyway, because my mother stopped correcting me all the time. My school year ended and my report card was not too bad, but not good enough for my mother. She complained to my stepfather, but he didn't criticize me one bit. Instead he told her to stop bitching and they had a fight again.

The school I had to go to was far from where we lived and to walk to school took some time. For the first week my mother walked with me but once I learned which way I had to go, she stopped taking me to school and I walked by myself. That was all right because I knew my way and arrived safely. It took forty-five to fifty minutes to walk, and only twenty minutes by streetcar but I could take the streetcar only when it was raining. On those occasions at the beginning, Mutti came with me to take me to school but later she would take me only to the streetcar stop. She would give me the exact fare money and would ask the conductor if he would be so kind as to let me off at Sonnenallee/Hersbergplatz, the stop I had to get off at to get to school. The conductor always promised by saying, "No problem, Mm. I will look after your little girl, don't worry." And later, most of them knew me, and my mother knew that I was in good hands. My school was located across from the stop and I just had to cross the street and had two more minutes to walk. And the way back home was not difficult because I knew our street and in the beginning my mother would pick me up from the stop anyway. Streetcars were marked by numbers. I had to take number 95, which would bring me to my school. So again, after we practiced the number at home and my mother was sure that I took the correct streetcar, she stopped taking me to the stop.

I spoke to my foster father

ONE RAINY DAY, I HAD MONEY FOR BOTH WAYS BUT LOST THE return fare and so I walked. It was raining but I didn't really care too much about getting wet. I was hopping along when suddenly I saw my foster father. I think he was on his way home because my foster parents didn't live too far away from my school. I was so excited that I forgot everything my mother had told me, such as, don't talk to strangers or if you ever see Herman or Meta don't go to them, etc. Instead, I ran after him and yelled out his name. He didn't turn at first and I was not sure if he heard me or saw me, so I continued to run after him and when I finally reached him, he stopped walking and yelled out, "Steffchen! [that's what they called me] It's you!" and he took me in his arms.

I think for a moment we both cried and after we stopped hugging, he pushed me away a little to have a better look at me. He looked surprised and told me how much I had grown and how pretty I had become. We walked for a while together but then he asked, "Where are you coming from?"

I told him that I lost my streetcar money and that I was walking home from school. He asked, "You are walking all by yourself?" and I proudly confirmed, "Yes, all by myself."

He looked at me still surprised and then said, "I will give you the money and will take you to the next stop." You must go home to your mother; she will be worried. And we can't be seen together, you understand?" He said this all in a very pronounced way and I understood what he was talking about. In my head I even heard my mother saying again, "Never talk to your foster parents."

However, I didn't want to stop talking to him nor did I want to go home yet. I wanted to stay with him and I didn't understand why he wanted me to go back to my mother so soon. He must have realized how unhappy I was, but still he knew that he couldn't help, so he told me that he would take me to the next streetcar stop. "That way," he said, "you will still be home on time and no harm is done."

"Just promise me that this will be our secret and that you will not tell your mother that we spoke together." I guess I had no choice but I couldn't really understand why it had to be like that. What was so wrong about talking just a little while longer? It felt so good to be close to him and I sure didn't want to part yet. I started to cry and begged him to just talk a little longer and then I asked him to take me to my foster mother, but he didn't give in.

It started to rain heavily now and we both got wet while we walked to the next stop. He held my hand and I cried but he went on walking and when I looked up, I saw my mother. She came towards us and I realized that she saw us too. I was paralyzed. I wanted to run but I couldn't and a moment later she stood in front of us and asked my foster father what he was doing here, with me, with her daughter. She then looked down to me and asked, "Are you all right?" And in her strict, unforgiving voice she carried on, asking, "Why are you with him? Where are you both coming from? Did he pick you up from school, or worse, did you not go to school at all? Answer me!"

But Herman answered for me, telling her where we found each other and then asking her, "Why is Steffie wandering around all by herself, Rosi? Shouldn't you be with her? Steffie is six years old. She should not go to school by herself, as a matter of fact, she should not be by herself, period. For your information, she lost her money for the streetcar and we saw each other by accident."

My mother didn't say a word, instead she just took my hand and we walked to the streetcar stop. My foster father stayed behind. I turned my head and I cried. The streetcar came and my mother told me to stop crying but I couldn't, I sobbed all the way home. I was not only sad, but also so scared because I knew what was ahead of me.

When we arrived home, she took me by my shoulders and shook me so hard that I thought my head would fall off. She screamed at me, "I told you not to speak to them, didn't I, but you can't listen, can you?" I answered truthfully that I met him and that we didn't talk long and that he was worried because I was walking alone. She looked at me in disgust and said, "Why didn't you take the streetcar in the first place?" And I had to tell her, again, that I lost the return fare. After hearing me out, she started to get more angry and she hit me right in my face. She didn't stop and she hit me again and again, and when she finally stopped she cried too but she told me how bad I was and that the best thing for me would be if she called the social worker again and had me picked up.

A neighbour knocked at the door and my mother went to answer it. The woman asked if everything was all right because she heard my crying but my mother assured her that everything was fine and closed the door quickly. When she returned, I was hiding under the bed but she pulled me out and wanted to start again; however, my stepfather came home and stopped her. My mother told him what I did, but he just said to me, "You didn't do anything wrong. You just said hello to your foster father and that is the right thing to do. After all he is not a stranger. The next time, however, try not to lose your money." And with that, the matter was closed.

After I was in bed, I heard my parents from the kitchen and I could make out that they were arguing and were having a big fight again.

Did my mother tell?

We had a knock at our door one day and when my mother opened it, two strange men were standing there. They exchanged a few words and she asked them to come in. They went straight to our room and talked for a while and she showed them some drawings. I didn't know what they were, but she talked about Papa and what he did at work. Again I didn't know what she was talking about but later she said to me that the men just did some checking about our apartment, and so I didn't worry about the strangers and didn't mention anything to Papa.

A few weeks later, we had just had dinner, Papa was reading the newspaper, and I was helping Mutti with the dishes, when somebody knocked. Mutti went to answer the door and when she opened it, two policemen were standing there asking if Papa was home. My mother didn't say anything but pointed with her hand to where they could find him. However, Papa must have heard something and came out of the room to see what was going on. Without many words they asked him for certain technical drawings and asked other questions I didn't understand.

After an hour or so they took Papa to the police station. Mutti didn't say a word about any of this but when

I asked her why they took Papa away, she just told me, "Because maybe he was bad and did something wrong." And she continued, saying, "This happens if you are bad, so you better watch out."

Of course I was so worried for Papa because I knew he was not bad at all.

A little later Wally came up and wanted to know what was going on. She told my mother that she saw the police coming down with my stepfather when she came home. She whispered to my mother, "Did you tell the police what you suspect he is doing?" But Mutti didn't answer and looked kind of funny towards me so Wally stopped asking. (Again, I didn't know what Wally meant and I asked my mother about it later but she just laughed and told me to forget it, it was a joke.)

After what seemed like a long time, my father came home and told my mother that as far as he was concerned, they thought he was a spy. "Not only are they wrong, but they have no proof." They took the drawings he worked on at home and told him to come back the next day to the station. He even laughed about it and said, "It is so ridiculous. As if I would leave anything I work on at home lying around if I were a spy. "You know too, Rosi, that I bring work home with me that I can't finish at work. What do they know about how busy we are at work? I have only two hands and it is hard to meet the deadlines. It is hard to be on time when everyone is drafted and they don't have enough personnel. If I had help, I wouldn't need to bring things home. Maybe somebody reported that I work at home, but who? Did you talk about it to somebody, maybe your friend Wally?" But my mother shook her head and answered that she never mentioned anything to anybody. He looked at her and said, now more to himself, "I really wonder how they found out that I work at home."

When my father came home the next day from work he told my mother that he didn't have to go back to the police station because the police were already at his work place, getting what they wanted from him before he came in. As he was told later by his boss, everything was taken care of. His company had explained what was going on and the police were satisfied. When I looked up, I saw disappointment in my mother's face, but when she spoke to my father she sounded happy for him.

I saw my foster parents

I THINK IT WAS IN THE SPRING OF 1943, WHEN I WAS IN BED
already for the evening and my parents were in our kitchen,
the sirens came on and we had to hurry down to the
shelter. Papa couldn't come with us; he was on duty that
night and in charge of checking the building in case phos-
phorus bombs came down and needed immediate attention. I was always scared when he was on watch because
he and other men had to go right on top of the roof to
watch our building. I cannot remember exactly why they
had to go onto the rooftop, but I was told that sometimes
these bombs didn't explode right away and the men had
to throw them down in a big tank, which most courtyards
had by now. The special tanks were built for that purpose, but they looked to me like swimming pools. If these
bombs exploded on top of the house, they would spread
fire so quickly that only immediate action would possibly
stop the rapid fire from burning the building down completely. The men were prepared to prevent whatever they
could and had these big water hoses ready in case they
were not able to get rid of the bomb in time. It was a very
dangerous job but they had to do it whether they wanted

to or not, and they could not come down until the alarm was cancelled.

It was a wild night, bombs were falling everywhere, and the Germans tried to shoot the planes down with cannons. Sometimes the walls of our shelter would sway and we were all scared but, again, we were lucky; our building was not hit. However, when we came out of the shelter and looked up at the sky, it was dark red towards the area where my foster parents lived, a sign that the area had been hit hard. My mother was so upset and started crying and when she saw Papa she told him that she had to see if my foster parents were all right. My stepfather asked at first quite cynically why she was so concerned, but she cried even more and said that she often thought about them now and wanted to check to see if they were OK. My father told her to leave me and go by herself but she wouldn't hear of it and insisted on taking me with her. At first he looked at her at in disbelief, but then he said, "Be careful and if there is another alarm, go into a shelter wherever you are. Hold Steffie's hand, don't let go of her. I would come with you, but they need my help here."

We walked for almost an hour because the street-cars were out of service and, of course, a taxi was out of the question; there were none to get. When we arrived, we couldn't believe what we saw; everything was up in flames. At first it looked as if the whole block had been hit by firebombs and it seemed as though there was no hope anymore and everything was destroyed. However, when we came a little closer, we saw that the side where my foster parents lived was somehow still intact and only half of the block was damaged and in flames. The fire department and all the people on duty worked like crazy to get trapped people out of the ruins. It was so awful and I was scared that my foster parents were among the wounded or, even worse, dead. We looked all over the place and at first thought for sure something had happened to them because we couldn't find them. Everything was closed off and we could not even get close to where they lived. My mother seemed so sad, saying almost to herself, "I hoped we would see them. I am so sorry for what I did to them." She cried now and we walked on, and just when we wanted to turn around to go home again, my foster mother saw us and came towards us.

She didn't say a word at first, but just took me in her arms. She looked at my mother somewhat sadly, but had a smile and wanted to know why we had come. My mother told her that she saw the sky from our house and was concerned and had to know if they were all right. Again, my foster mother started to smile and said, "Are you sure that's the reason or are you in trouble?" And in the same breath she continued, "How is your marriage? I see you are not pregnant, is everything all right?"

My mother didn't answer her questions. Instead she repeated, "I just came to see if you were OK because as I said, from our street we could see that your area was bombed hard. The sky was so dark red that I was scared that something had happened to you." My foster father came and joined us.

He, too, took me up and gave me a hug and a kiss. He looked dirty and was full of dust and soot. He said that they had tried to keep the fire under control but it was too much and before the fire department came, most of that one part was burned down. And then he looked at my mother and asked her the same question, "What are you doing here?"

But before my mother answered, my foster mother explained, "Rosi was worried about us. She saw the sky and came." And with that, the conversation ended.

I was so happy to see both my Mutti and Papa because that's what they still were to me. I really didn't mind the fire, as long they were OK and I could be close to them. My foster father had to go back again. He gave me a big hug and a kiss and with tears in his eyes he said, "Take care of yourself, Steffchen. I am so glad you came." And then he left us.

Soon after he left, my mother said that we must hurry back home too because Richard would be worried. My foster mother thanked her for coming and took me up into her arms and said, more to me than to my mother, "Come back, we miss you so much."

And when I told her that I missed her too, I started to cry. I said to my mother, "I don't want to go home, I want to stay with Mutti."

But my mother said, "We must go. We will be back, I promise." We hugged again, even my mother gave Mutti a kiss and then we left. It was the last time that I saw my foster father.

We came home early in the morning, and as it started to get light outside, we could see the true damage. There were ruins everywhere. Many people were crying and ambulances were making this terrible noise, almost like the sirens did before we had to go into the shelter. We were both crying by now, I because I had to leave my foster parents behind and my mother because she was sad too. I didn't know why but, after all, she was the one who had needed to see my foster parents. She carried me for a while because we were both so tired and exhausted, and when we arrived at our apartment, my mother put me into my bed right away and said to me, "At least you saw them again. I realize that you still love them so much and who knows what lies ahead of us." And then she gave me a kiss. I was too tired to feel much but I must have been happy somehow because I fell asleep as soon she closed the door.

We were evacuated to Poland

SHORTLY AFTER THAT NIGHT, MY MOTHER TOLD ME THAT WE would go on a trip. She said, "We will leave Papa for a while and move to the country." As she explained to me, there would be no bombs and no sirens and we would be safe. "You will see, it will be fun." Right away I asked why Papa was not coming with us, but Mutti answered, "He has to work. Don't worry, he will visit us often." I also asked if I could take my doll, the one I always brought with me, and if she would take her piano. Mutti laughed and told me that I could take my doll but she would have to leave her piano behind. She explained, "We will not stay long. Surely the war will be over soon and then we will come home again."

"Do I still have to go to school," I asked.

"Oh, yes," she answered, "you must go to school, but this will be all right. You will make new friends, and so will I. Don't worry, everything will be fine."

My mother seemed changed, she didn't slap me as often anymore and she didn't tell me that I had to go to reform school when I did something wrong, so I thought that maybe she wasn't so bad after all. Yes, my mother seemed to be happy, and in a way Papa seemed to be too. At least they didn't fight as often anymore.

A few days later, my stepfather came home with a lot of documents that he and Mutti filled out and the following week Mutti packed two suitcases, one for her and a smaller one for me and Papa took us to the train station. We took a taxi, my first time in a car.

I still remember how excited I was when we arrived at the train station. I didn't really realize what was happening. There were so many people and screams and whistles, not to mention the tears. There were soldiers and girls hugging, saying their good-byes, and families like us. Of course it was exciting.

Papa took me up, hugged me and told me to be good, and he promised to visit soon. "Be brave," he whispered to me. I didn't know what he meant but I promised that I would and I gave him a hug back. Even my mother had tears in her eyes and they hugged too.

And then we boarded the train and a few minutes later whistles blew and with a big push we were moving. We had a window seat and my mother took me up and I saw my Papa waving and we waved back and then suddenly we couldn't see him anymore, and the train station became smaller and smaller and soon it was gone.

I thought, of course, that it was a fun trip but I learned later that Hitler actually evacuated all mothers and children to the East, speculating that he wouldn't be overrun by Russia. In other words, he felt safe and secure on the Eastern Front, at least at the time these evacuations took place. Our destination was Poland, Szubin, or as they called it in German, Alt Burgund, approximately 300 km away from Berlin. It was a little town situated between Bydgoszes or then Bromberg and Pozuan, translated in German, Posen. The area was more or less all farmland and during the war, it was Hitler's food source for Germany.

We arrived late at night and were welcomed by the Gauleiter, the mayor of the city, and a few other important people. They were all dressed in their uniforms and looked like officers, strict and proper, but nevertheless friendly. There was a whole group of us, mothers and children, and we all were tired but, of course, the first question was, where would we stay for the few months we planned to be in Poland? But the mayor and his people told everybody to calm down until the morning. He said, "The first night you will all sleep in our school and after that we will find suitable quarters for everybody, I promise. We will look after you and I am sure you will like it here."

So the first night we were escorted to a nearby school gym. We were given a meal and could wash up but then we had to sleep on the floor. I was homesick already and wanted to go back home, but my mother told me to wait until the next morning when everybody would be placed in the home of a family. She said, "At least we will have our own room, just wait, it will all be all right." She smiled and assured me that everything would be fine and sure enough, after we had breakfast, our name was called and my mother was told that they had a place for us at a farm. I think Mutti was not too excited about that; she would have preferred to stay in town, but we could not choose where we wanted to stay and had to take what was offered to us.

We had to wait for quite a while but by late afternoon our name was called again and we were directed towards a young man who took our suitcases and guided us to a little coach that had two horses in front of it. He was very courteous, introduced himself, helped us to get into the coach and gave us blankets to cover our legs. I found this all very exciting, but my mother was a little skeptical. She asked the young man how far we would go out of town and he answered in broken German that it would take about one and a half hours or so. I giggled about the way he spoke to us but Mutti explained to me that he was a Pole and couldn't speak much German. She said, "You mustn't laugh about the way he talks. I think it is pretty good that he speaks both Polish and a bit of German."

Of course I didn't really understand what she was talking about but I stopped my giggling. When we were safely seated and he thought we were comfortable, he took his place in the front, gave the horses a little click with his tongue, and off we went. For me this was all very exciting but I was still tired from the night before and soon fell asleep. My mother woke me up when we arrived. It was late by now. The farmer, who was very young, came toward us and introduced himself and they shook hands. He, too, was very polite and spoke German but it sounded different than what we spoke in Berlin. However, I could understand him and when he bent down to me and asked me how old I was, I found him very pleasant. He showed us the way into his house and we met his wife, who was even younger than he was. She carried a baby in her arm and told us that this was their nine-month-old son. It was rather dark in the house since they had no electricity, but I noticed that it was dirty there and I whispered something about it to my mother, who whispered back to me telling me to be quiet. I wondered why my mother didn't see the dirt because she was a clean freak and surely must have noticed it as well. Anyway, I was too tired by now to carry on and wanted to go to sleep. When they showed us our room I forgot the dirt and wanted to go straight to bed. However, we saw only one bed and were told that they had only one bed for us and that we would have to sleep together. We were both not crazy about the idea, but what could we do, we were both too tired to argue. We also learned that there was no running water in the house but only a basin and beside it a pitcher with water. The bathroom was outside and so was the water pump. (My mother had been told before we arrived that we would have a very comfortable room waiting for us.)

The farmer and his wife asked us to join them for supper and my mother agreed and thanked them for the invitation. I was not hungry but my mother told me to at least eat something, so after we cleaned ourselves up a little, we went to the kitchen. We both realized that our lives had changed. Everything was different here: no running water, no electricity, and no bathroom. The toilet was outside and for toilet paper they had newspapers cut in little squares. My mother told me to rub the paper first between my hands before I used it. She explained that it would make it softer. When we finally went to our room and lay down in the bed, we realized that the mattress was a sack of straw, but we were both so tired, we didn't care; at least not for this night, our first night in a little dark room, away from home, which wasn't much either, but much better than what we had here.

We had arrived on a weekend so my mother could not do much about our lodgings but she was not happy and said that she would go to the Gauleiter on Monday and would try to get something in the city or at least close to it, because this was too far out and too far away from everything.

The next day when I was looking around, I actually thought it was neat there because wherever I went there was something new to see and to do. Too bad they didn't have older children I could play with, just the little baby who actually cried a lot. Mutti said the baby was sore and had diaper rash. She told me that she saw it and it was really a shame; no wonder the little guy was unhappy.

Sunday night my mother asked our landlord how she could get a ride to the city because she wanted to talk to the Gauleiter. Our landlord looked surprised and asked if we didn't like it at his place, but my mother was polite and said, "No, it's not that, but I have some questions and must talk to him. Also," she continued, "if we stay here my daughter has to go to school and I have to enroll her since she missed almost one week already. I hope," she carried on, "they have a school close by." The farmer, somewhat calmer because at first he seemed upset, told her that there was a bus going to the city twice a day. So if she got up early she would be able to catch the first one and have a chance to return the same day. Mother made sure that we made it to town in time so that she could talk to the Gauleiter.

I cannot remember too much but I know that we stayed on the farm for a few weeks and the school was forty-five minutes away. There was no transportation to the school and I had to walk back and forth with a whole bunch of other kids. At first it was fun but later I hated it and often got into trouble. We were all in one room; the younger kids were at the front and the older kids sat in the back. Since we were so much more advanced with our curriculum in Berlin, I was ahead of everybody in my class but the teacher refused to advance me so I was bored.

I was also often teased because I was a city kid and was called a sissy because I complained a lot and hated the long walks back and forth to school. And I spoke with a different dialect, so there was more teasing since everybody thought it sounded very funny. To defend myself I told everybody who wanted to listen, that we were going home to the big city soon. They often asked me why I came in the first place. I was not a happy camper but my mother couldn't and wouldn't help. She always told me to behave but I told her I hated the place and I wanted to go home.

Soon Papa came to visit us and we had a few nice days together. By the way, he went with Mutti to the town office and within a short while we had a room in town and moved. He came to help us move our stuff, which wasn't much, but Mutti was glad that he was with us. There were no fights between them and I was happy that Papa came to visit. I didn't want him to leave us, but soon he told me he had to go back to work. He promised me that he would be back soon. We went together to the train station and when we said our good-byes I gave him a big hug and told him that I sure missed him and he told me that he missed me too.

Our new room was nice. It was small and located on the second floor, almost under the roof. The house was big and belonged to Herr Mueller, the owner of the local drugstore/dispensary. Herr Mueller was drafted and, I was told, helped to win the war. The store, which was located beside the front entrance of the house, was run by his wife and another woman who managed the dispensary. I forgot the woman's name but I later learned to dislike her because she always told on me when I did something wrong or was mischievous.

The Muellers lived on the main floor with their bedrooms on the first floor. Frau Mueller's father lived on the second floor, where we now had a room too. It was a beautiful house. I had never seen so many nice things in my whole life and I admired the rich furniture. Unfortunately I was not allowed to touch anything, only to look at things. Our room was not too bad either. We had a rather nice view into the backyard and the furniture was much better than ours at home. The best part was that we had a washroom all to ourselves and central heating. Once in a while I even had a bath in the big bathtub, but most times my mother put me in a big wash bowl and would scrub me from head to toe. As she said, we must save water and heat. The Muellers also had a third floor, but I never went there. Compared to the farm this was heaven; it was even better than at home, where we only had a toilet without a bathtub.

The Muellers had a daughter named Renate. She was a bit older than I was and was very pretty. We played together a lot, but she often told me to do or to get things that got me into trouble while she went free. Her grandfather, who was called Opa by everybody, often took my side because he realized what Renate was doing; however my mother was still upset with me and sometimes spanked me for things I didn't do at all. It surely was not fair that Renate got away with things I am sure I wouldn't have, but she was the only kid close by that I could play with. She was spoiled rotten and could never do anything wrong in the eyes of her mother. I had no choice other than to keep on playing with her or get bored.

I was going to a new school again. The school was not too far from where we lived and the teacher was nice. I got better marks than in Berlin and Mutti was happy about that. She was much nicer to me of late and I felt happy about it. Since our move to Alt Burgund, Papa, who came every second week, seemed happy too. And another thing I realized was that I hardly thought about my foster parents anymore. Everything was so far away and actually so peaceful here that I probably had no reason to be sad.

One day Mutti told me that we might have a baby. Because Mutti was so happy about it and Papa was beside himself when he heard the news, I was happy too. Everything seemed fine until one morning Mutti was crying and told me that the baby was not coming; as she said, it was a false alarm. She said, "I got my period this morning and so, we will have no baby." I asked her what a period was and she explained to me that one day I will have this too. I think this was my first sex lesson, the only one by the way, since most of the time nobody talked about the facts of life. Of course I was confused by all this; first we were going to have a baby then we were not going to have a baby. I guess Mutti was very upset. However the worst thing was, she started to get mean again and whatever I did, it was wrong. She was upset about almost everything, and when Papa came and she told him that there would be no baby, he too was not very happy. Later that night they even had a fight and when he left, he hardly said good-bye to her, but still gave me a big hug and told me to hang in there.

Mutti's leg also became bad again and for a few weeks

she had to go to the hospital and I had to stay with our landlady and with Renate. I can't remember much about it, but I know that when Mutti came back I started to remember my foster parents again and knew that this was a bad sign. Also, my stepfather didn't come to visit too often anymore; instead he sent telegrams saying that he had to work. As a matter of fact, he didn't come for weeks and Mutti, who had a new girlfriend, said to her that Papa had another woman in Berlin. She told her that Papa had her before we left but stopped seeing her for a while. However now she was almost certain that they had started seeing each other again.

Her new girlfriend, whose husband was in the war, told Mutti that she was probably wrong because from what she heard, everybody who was not drafted had to work as much as they could so that Germany would win the war. My mother was not too sure and rather wanted to believe that my stepfather had this woman whom he had had for a long time.

When Mutti's leg was better again she took a course to become a Red Cross nurse. The course was in Bromberg, quite a way from where we lived. So she left me with our landlady and Renate again and I didn't mind. I didn't see Mutti for weeks and was quite happy with Renate and I learned to love her grandfather.

In the fall of 1943 the war was not much in favor of Germany anymore. Italy crumbled and capitulated to the Allies in September, and on October 13th declared war on Germany. The Germans were, of course, bitter and called it treason. Also in October, the Red Army gained ground on Hitler's once greatest Eastern Front and took away the safe feeling the German people had in Poland. The homeland of Germany was bombarded with great force now and it was almost clear that the Allies would have the upper hand some way or another not too far in the future.

My mother came back from her course in a brand-new German Red Cross uniform and I thought she looked great. She worked now in the town's small hospital and after school I had to go to a kindergarten, where they served meals and looked after children whose parents were working, etc. I liked it there because I knew many kids from school. The "aunts" were nice also and I never felt alone. (We had to call the social workers "aunts" rather than Mrs. or Miss.)

However when the kindergarten closed at night and my mother had to work late, I went home and had to stay by myself or sometimes played with Renate. One after-noon I came home and an ambulance was in front of our house. I ran up to our apartment because I thought something was wrong with my mother, but it was Renate they carried out. Her Opa told me that she had become very sick the night before and the doctor wanted her to stay in the hospital because of the high fever. A day or so later my mother told me that Renate was never coming home again. She had died of scarlet fever. I was so sad and confused because I was not sure what really happened to her, other than that she would never come back and I would miss her. I realized that she was my best girlfriend. Her mother cried for a month and her Opa was also so very sad and I guess that's why I became so close to him. I kind of became his Renate.

I had to stay home at first because people thought I was infected too, but I guess I was lucky. I didn't get it and everybody was relieved. My stepfather came to visit us again. He stayed a few days and it was a nice visit because my parents didn't fight at all. However they were very sad in a way because Papa told us how bad it was now in Berlin. He told us that most of the houses were in ruins and that we would lose the war, hopefully, as he said, soon. Our apartment building was still standing, but we had lost all the windows and he just closed them with boards and wood. The apartment was bitter cold because the ration for the coal shipment was shortened again. The store that sold coal had run out of inventory. There was wood from the ruins, but it didn't do much for the *Kachelofen* and actually, if you were caught taking the wood, it was considered stealing and you could go to jail for it. Papa said to us, "Be glad you are here, at least you can still sleep at night and you are warm."

Our good-byes were sad this time because we didn't know when, and if, we would see each other again. For the first time I kind of understood that we were at war and that it was a bad time we lived in. That winter of 1943/44 was cold and long and people were worn out and sad.

I started to grow and my clothes were either too small or too big. One day my mother had to travel all the way to Bromberg to get a nice winter coat for me. Mutti picked it up without me trying it on because if the stores had a new shipment, people literally stormed the store and you had to be quick to get anything from the shelves at all. I guess my mother was lucky that she was able to get this coat for me, and I, even though I didn't like it much, was lucky to get a new coat at this time. Oh yes, the coat was much too big for me, and I was glad at first that I was not allowed to wear it because, as she said, it was too good to be worn. But later, when I was allowed to wear it, this coat became the only good possession I had and of course nobody knew what the coat and I would go through together.

The summer of '44 was boring for me because I missed Renate and I was on my own a lot. My mother went to work and my days were always the same: in the morning I went to school, after school I had to go to kindergarten where I had supper and later, when I walked home, into our little room, I was alone again, waiting for my mother who was sometimes very late. Too often I just put myself to bed and fell asleep. At times Frau Mueller or Opa would take me down to sit with them, but since Renate died it was not the same anymore and I felt very uncomfortable with them. It was different when I was alone with Opa because he played cards or checkers with me. And I could talk to him about many things or I could ask him questions, questions I certainly could never ask my mother. He was a nice person and I knew he liked me too.

One day in school we were vaccinated and the next day I didn't feel well. My arm was swollen and all red and my mother told me to stay in bed. She made a sandwich for me and told me that there was some lemonade for me, and then she left. I fell asleep again and woke up because I was so hot and I felt sick to my stomach. I had a little pee pot under my bed and was able to use it to throw up without making a mess. I was so weak by now that I hardly could get back to my bed, but I made it and fell back asleep. I woke up with a bad headache and felt really thirsty but didn't want to drink the lemonade. I got a glass of water and must have passed out because when I woke up I was in my bed again and Opa was sitting right beside me. I had different pajamas on and he told me that he had changed them because my other ones were damp from sweat. He spoke but I couldn't understand what he was talking about because the room went around and around and I was hot and my bedspread felt like I was touching a stone. A bit later the doctor came and the first thing he asked was where my mother was. Opa answered that she was at work and should be home soon. The doctor told him that I was burning up with fever and never should have been left alone. Anyway, just as he was speaking to Opa, my mother came in. The doctor gave her an earful. He said that I had a bad reaction and never should have been left without care. He left soon and Opa told my mother that at least she should have let him know; it was just by accident that he heard when I fell and he looked in on me. When he left, my mother started crying and blamed me for having made a big fuss but she didn't leave me alone again when I didn't feel well.

I got better after a few days but felt guilty that I had gotten sick.

The end is near,
we have to flee

THE WAR GOT WORSE AND EVERYBODY WAS NERVOUS AND ANX-
ious. Everybody knew that the war was lost except Hitler
and his gang; they wanted to fight to the end. In late fall
of 1944 my mother was told that she might be drafted to
go to the front. She phoned my stepfather at work and he
told her that he would try to get her off but he couldn't
promise of course. He asked her what she would do with
me and she told him that the government would take care
of me but Frau Mueller had promised to look after me so
she would probably leave me here. "You know, Richard,"
I heard her saying, "it is out of my control. That is why
I am phoning you. Maybe you can help. Don't you have
connections?"

He must have been upset with her because she stopped
talking about me and asked, "How is it in Berlin?"

"Don't even ask." my stepfather said, "Be glad that
you are still safe."

She hung up and told me later that Papa sounded a bit
angry when she phoned him, but what else could she have
done? Anyway, my stepfather was not able to help but she

never got the draft papers anyway and so she worried for nothing. I really didn't understand what was going on, all I knew was that I wasn't left alone again or left to stay with Frau Mueller.

Shortly after my ninth birthday, on a cold January day in 1945, a bunch of German soldiers came to the house and asked if they could stay overnight. Frau Mueller gave them a room and later invited them to come down for a meal and a drink. She also came up to see my mother and I guess she invited her down too. My mother declined the meal but went down soon after I was in bed. Before she left, she kissed me and said, "I will be back soon, so sleep well."

I woke up from the noise and the loud music. At first I didn't know where it came from, but then I remembered and realized it came from downstairs, from the soldiers. I jumped out of my bed and went straight down to see what was going on.

They were having a party, everybody was drunk and wild and they were dancing and kissing. I had never seen anything like it. Even Frau Mueller spoke funny. However, I couldn't see my mother and so I started to look for her. I found her in one of the bedrooms with two soldiers. They were all drunk and naked. One soldier was on top of Mutti and I thought he wanted to kill her, so I screamed out, "What are you doing to my mother?"

The other soldier, who was standing a bit back and looked like he was watching them, said in a very funny tone, "They are fucking!" And he laughed as loud as he could. Of course I didn't know what he was talking about and wanted to go closer to see what was going on when Opa came running into the room and took me by my arm and pulled me out to the hall.

He looked very sad and mumbled, saying, "Oh my God, you shouldn't have gone into the room, what can I tell you, what can I tell you?"

I looked up at him and asked him, "Opa, what is fucking?"

Obviously he was shocked, but he answered with a straight face that it was playing around and I must have been satisfied with the explanation because when he told me to go back to our room, I went back to bed and fell asleep again.

When I woke up the next morning my mother was already up. The soldiers were gone; the house was still again. Mutti looked awful and sad. I didn't know if she knew what I had seen but she didn't say anything other than that I had to get up quickly because we had to go away from here as soon as we could. She continued, saying that the Russians were already close to the Polish border. "So get up and get dressed. You have to help me with the packing. We will leave in two or three hours."

I didn't understand a word but did what she asked me to do, got up and got dressed.

I asked why we had to leave and she just said, "Don't ask, just help me with the packing."

Mutti was nervous and cried. She filled the suitcases, packed and unpacked and always said that we could only take this or that and had to leave most of our belongings behind. She told me that I had to put on two to three layers of clothing because we would be on Opa's big wagon with his horse to pull us. And of course Frau Mueller was coming too. "They are so kind to take us along. Opa will lead the horse."

I asked her again why we had to go so soon and this

time she answered and said that the German soldiers had told them that the Russians would be here within a few days and we should run and flee back to Berlin.

"Do we take the dog?"

"I guess so," my mother said, "but I am not sure."

"Do we have to leave today?" I asked again, because it didn't make sense to me at all that we had to do what these soldiers, who were so rowdy last night, had said. But my mother just said, "Put your clothes on but put your new coat under the old one and take your new shoes. I will pack the old shoes in your suitcase. Take three pairs of gloves and put three pairs of stockings on." (We kids had these ugly thick stockings which were held up with a rubber band, tied up by buttons and connected to a little undershirt.)

I hated these stockings in the first place and now I had to put on three pairs? No way, and at once, without thinking, I objected, "I can't tie up three pairs of stockings!" But Mutti just looked at me with her funny look and I did what she told me to do. She helped me a bit and I managed the rest. It felt funny to wear three pairs of stockings but the nice part was, my new shoes did fit now, they were not too big anymore.

Two hours later Opa knocked on the door and asked us if we were ready because the horse was harnessed and Ossi (Oswald), the German Shepherd, was waiting. Mutti looked around and told him that all she still had to do was get dressed herself but other than that we were ready and we would come down in about five minutes. I felt like a fat snowman; I could hardly move with all my clothes on and I started to complain that I was hot, so Mutti told me to go down already. "Don't run away or fall into the snow. I will be down too, just give me a few more minutes."

I took my doll and went down. Frau Mueller started to climb up into the wagon. She turned around and asked why my mother was not ready yet, but before I could explain, my mother came out of the door and Opa closed and locked the door after her. He turned the key very slowly and we were all sad, but we did not have much time and climbed onto the wagon, which Opa had filled up with straw. We certainly did not have much room to move but it kept us warm. We all had a lot of clothes on and on top of her layers my mother wore the Red Cross uniform.

Opa looked at her and asked her if it was necessary to wear the uniform but my mother just said, "It's in case I can help should somebody need me."

We drove out of town and met up with others and soon we had a wagon train of about twenty all together. The weather was cold and it started to snow again. On our way we met many German soldiers who told us to hurry because the end of the war was near and who knew what the enemy had in store for us. They all looked as if they had given up a long time ago but couldn't do anything about it. The fight had to go on until the end. Some said they wished they could flee with us. "God be with you." And we returned the wish and said, "And also with you."

Off and on we heard noises like thunder and all of us were scared and we cuddled together. But my old doll gave me the most comfort. I was so glad that my mother had allowed me to take her with us because I knew how she hated her. Often the whole wagon train came to a standstill because we entered a battle zone and we were bombarded by rifles, cannons and even planes. We had to make detours and were blocked by soldiers, trucks, and tanks. We passed villages where dead people were lying all over the roads and where the houses were still burning from a previous battle. Many farm animals were running like the people, in all directions. It was awful and our whole group was in chaos but we all had to go on. For two days we made stops only to feed the horses and give them water.

Before we left home, Opa had taken a big pail with him so we could go to the washroom without stopping the wagon. Even the grownups used it. We emptied it either when we all stopped or while we were still driving. We just had one thing in our mind and that was to get away from the Russians and stay alive.

After almost two days without much sleep, Opa got so tired that he couldn't go on anymore. I think we were almost the only wagon without a backup driver. Frau Mueller had never learned how to handle a horse and my mother was of course a city girl. Anyway, this did not help our situation, because Opa needed to sleep. He mentioned our situation to others and shortly after we had another Opa who steered the horse as well as our Opa did. Our Opa came to the back of the wagon and, with Ossi beside him, fell asleep instantly.

By the way, Ossi, a beautiful German Shepherd, had become very nervous. Quite often he jumped off the wagon and hardly listened to Opa anymore, which made it hard to hold onto him and Opa was not very pleased with him. Before he had been so obedient but now he hardly listened. Frau Mueller said he should have left him at home, but Opa didn't want to hear about it at all and answered, "Ossi is nervous, maybe he knows more than we do. I hope it isn't a bad sign."

We halted again and found out that there was a school close by and that we could stay there overnight. Some didn't want to stop but many decided that it was needed and so, after the horses were looked after, we went inside and were greeted by the people of the little town. We received our first warm meal since we left Alt Burgund and got warm again. The three layers of clothes didn't help much in minus twenty degree weather and we were all half frozen. My feet already had some frostbite and all of us had almost stiff hands. When my mother looked at my feet and an old woman saw them, she suggested that my mother pee in a pot and put my feet into the warm pee. I protested, of course, but my mother made me do it and you know what, it helped.

Anyway, we were not too far away from the German border anymore and the next day, very early in the morning, we carried on with our journey. We were somehow all refreshed and warm and the world looked much better to us after the rest.

When we had left, many people from the town joined us, but some stayed back and wished us all the best. Nobody knew what our future would bring and whether we would all make it, but we kids really didn't know why we had to be here in the first place and why this was all happening to us. We were scared and helpless and hung onto our mothers or Opas, because most fathers were not with us; they were in the war, still fighting for a lost cause.

We were about a hundred kilometers from Schneide-muehl at the German border when Ossi wanted to jump down again. Opa couldn't hold him back and had to let him go. About two minutes later we heard shots and a long howl. Obviously it was Ossi who had been shot, because this time he didn't come back. Opa called him, and called him again and again, but his beloved dog never returned and we had to leave him behind. We were all sad and Opa started to cry. Ossi meant so much to him and now he was gone. After a while we got over the big loss and shock but we started to wonder who shot Ossi and why? Who would kill such a beautiful dog in the first place? Maybe he became aggressive? He never was before. But it was too late to think about all of that; he was gone.

An hour or so later we knew who shot him because now we became the target. Russian partisans, dressed in German uniforms, came so close to us that we could see them and actually wave to them, when suddenly they opened fire on us. We came to a halt and many of us jumped off the wagons but these partisans, who we thought were German soldiers, stopped shooting and after a minute or so they were gone and the forest and the road were quiet again. Everybody was confused because of the uniforms, but some people saw them showing the Soviet flag before they moved on and we knew then that they were Russians.

After we recovered from this new drama we continued our journey, but everybody was worried. It was bitter cold and started to snow. We were all tired and the horses needed food, but nobody wanted to stop. I think everybody thought that maybe in just a day or a bit longer we would be back in Germany and we could have all the rest needed. Even so everybody was worried; we all hoped that we would make it, so nobody wanted to stop yet.

At one point, after a short break, Opa was at the reins

again and my mother was sitting beside him. He told her to take off her Red Cross uniform. He said to her that if the Russians were to find us, she would be the first to go. "Rosi, if they need nurses and they see you are one, they will take you. Believe me and listen, take the stupid uniform off." And because I was so scared that these people would take her and I would be all alone, I agreed with Opa and begged her to listen to him. After a moment, she crawled to the back and changed. Opa smiled and said, "That's better."

Not long after my mother took off her uniform, about fifty kilometers or so from the German border, the wagon train came to a halt again. Opa asked what was wrong this time and tried to find out by leaning out to see better what was going on and why we had stopped again. But since we were near the end of the caravan, nobody knew exactly until we heard shots. About a minute later we saw soldiers, but not German ones, that was for sure. Somebody whispered, "They're Russians." And again in a whisper, "My God, these are Russian soldiers!"

A minute later we were all ordered to get down and were told with sign language, loud comments in Russian, which we couldn't understand, and with gunshots, which we understood very well, to build a big circle.

Children were crying and their mothers held onto them and hushed them to stop because they didn't want to bring extra attention onto themselves. We could all see that these soldiers had no patience and nobody knew what they would do to us. We learned very quickly! People who had dogs beside them were told to step out of the ring. Then with a big smile on his face, a soldier went in front of them and shot the dogs. Just like that, without a blink.

Nobody could think straight anymore. We all stood there like cattle. The soldiers came around and we were ordered to put our hands behind our heads. They patted us up and down, looking for weapons. They asked questions we did not understand, but if we didn't reply, we were hit with a rifle. It was a terrible situation. Many of us started praying but were told, more or less in sign language, that if we didn't stop, we would be shot.

There were about thirty soldiers. They all looked dirty and many had ripped uniforms. Most soldiers were very young and cocky but some were middle-aged and looked tired and worn-out.

They made the round in threes; one pointed a pistol towards the person who was being investigated and searched for weapons, the second told the person to line up across from the circle, and the third soldier watched that the orders were properly followed.

Three men were shot right away, because two still wore their NSDAP (Hitler's party) buttons on their coats, and one had a gun. My mother whispered, "So stupid, how could they!" Right away a soldier looked at us, but didn't say anything.

The circle became smaller and smaller. A family—father, mother and a small baby—was told to stay and didn't have to join the lines yet. When the three soldiers came over to us, another one joined them. He looked in some way better and cleaner than the others and we learned later that he was an officer. He bent down to have a better look at me and asked in broken German if I was Jewish. Because my mother didn't understand exactly what he was talking about, she said *Ja* (yes). He looked again and waved our group over to go back to our wagon and told us to wait there.

The officer went back to the family who was told to remain in the circle. I can't remember the reason why they were told not to join the others, but I heard their baby crying. Anyway, they too were told by the officer to go back to their wagon and wait.

The Russian soldiers were finished with sorting us out and everyone except the four of us and the other group were lined up. There were so many people in the line. Children were crying and we were all nervous, not knowing what would happen next. Two or three soldiers went to the lined-up group and looked for watches, rings, and other fine jewelry. Some people didn't want to part with their jewelry, especially women who didn't want to give up their wedding rings. They protested but there was no mercy and they too were threatened that they would be shot if they didn't hand everything over.

They stopped taking away the jewelry when the officer who told us to go back to our wagon returned and walked towards the line of people. He looked around and then gave some orders to his soldiers.

All the soldiers stood at attention but soon after divided again in groups of three as they had before. They then marched the people towards a big windmill, which we saw in the distance. They made them more or less run rather than walk. It was a sad scene.

Our group didn't move, we just looked on in horror and had to wait in front of our wagons, two lonely scared groups asking ourselves why we couldn't also go to the shelter. Because that was what all of us thought, that they were being guided to a shelter, which we assumed the windmill was. We watched but after a while the group became smaller and smaller in the distance and then they disappeared.

I was so cold by now that I couldn't move anymore. I didn't cry or say a word, I was just shivering and Opa came closer to me to shelter me from the strong wind and the snow. My teeth made a terrible noise and I was worried that the soldiers would hear it but I was not able to control anything anymore and to top it all off, I peed my pants. In no time my wet clothes froze and I was even colder.

The officer, along with a few other soldiers, came back to us. They stood more or less beside us and watched with their binoculars as the long line disappeared into the windmill.

A few minutes went by and we thought that they would shoot us because we had to stay behind and they moved a bit away from us and pointed their guns towards us. We all were sure that this was the end, but they didn't shoot, instead they pointed their hand back to the windmill. We understood that they wanted to show us something. We tried harder so see what they meant and then we saw it. The windmill was on fire. It was burning! They burned the people alive. We all screamed and cried out loudly, and couldn't believe what we saw, what had happened, but they forced us to watch this terrible drama. The fire was now so high that we knew that all of the people who had shared the few days with us, who were all innocent and just wanted to get out of the dilemma we were in, had been killed within half an hour or so. They burned them alive and without mercy and I never ever will forget what they made us witness, not as long as I live.

The officer turned back to us and in his broken German told us to return from where we had come and to tell everybody who wanted to flee what had happened. And then he said, "I hope you will make it back because not everybody is as merciful as I am."

We all climbed back onto the wagons as quickly as we could and thanked God that we were still alive.

Opa could hardly move and had problems breathing, so Frau Mueller took the reins and with Opa's directions, she steered the horse. She surprised all of us because she did really well. The other wagon followed us until we were stopped again, this time by German soldiers. They wondered why we were coming from the wrong direction and were concerned that we had gotten lost, but when we explained what happened, they were surprised and worried because they realized that they were practically surrounded on all sides and they should give themselves up.

It was getting dark and Opa suggested that we should stop and give the horse the last little bit of food we still had for him. The horse looked so tired and I felt sorry for him. Opa got out of the wagon and told us to eat a little as well. The other people agreed and joined us. Soon Opa fed the horse and collected snow in a pail for water. He made a very small fire and held the pail over it and after a few minutes, it worked; he had water for all three horses.

The other people fed their horses as well. They still had enough fodder and offered to share some for our horse, which Opa gladly accepted. They were kind people and wondered why they were spared and still alive as well. We all were in shock and couldn't stop crying. It came over us in waves, some of us would stop and some would start crying again.

After a while I asked my mother if all these people who were burned were now in heaven, but my mother answered that she was not sure how quick our dear God could work. However, she was sure that after a while they would all meet there again. I was a bit skeptical and asked, "Everybody goes to heaven, the bad people too?"

"Well," she answered, "No, I don't think so, but that's why it takes longer. It is up to God of course, but because he has sent us his son Jesus Christ, I believe almost everybody will be forgiven and will go to heaven. I am sure that one day we will all meet again." That explanation made sense to me and I was much more at ease again. I was still scared, but I thought it was not too bad, because for sure by now they should all be in heaven.

The next afternoon, I guess, we were close to where we had come from. I can't remember, but we must have passed the school we had stayed overnight in two nights ago. I didn't recognize it, but my mother pointed her finger saying, "Isn't this the school where we stayed?"

"I guess it is," Opa answered, "but it is burned down now."

From not too far away we heard gun shots, rumbling, and noises that frightened us again, and we realized that we were close to a battle zone. We hurried to get through without being detected, and after we passed it, Opa said, "If all goes well, we should be back in Alt Burgund and home by tomorrow afternoon."

He was steering the horse and the people behind us made sure that they stayed close so that we wouldn't get separated. Once in a while we heard their baby cry, but I guess its mother made sure to quiet it down again. She was worried, because the baby had a bit of a fever.

We were all so cold and longed for food and shelter. The snow was falling heavily and it started to get much colder again and Frau Mueller stared to laugh and said to Opa that he should stop at the next café because she needed her hot cup of coffee and a piece of cake. Opa answered and joked back saying, "We will be there in a few minutes or so, Ma'am." At first I believed them because I asked, "Really?" Later I realized it was just a joke and somehow I was disappointed.

A bit later, as I remember, we were stopped by German soldiers again and when they tried to talk to us, we heard shots being fired all around us and we all went down as low as we could, right into the straw on the wagon. I held onto my doll and was scared that this time we would get killed for sure. When we looked up again, the German soldiers were gone and the Russians were so close, we could see them. They spotted us too and within a minute or so we were surrounded and had to get off our wagons. Again, we had to put our arms up with hands behind our head. Since I still had my doll in my arms I had to let her go and she fell down. A Russian soldier picked her up, cleaned the snow off her, gave her back to me and showed me with a gesture that I was allowed to keep my arms down. He went to the horse, looked at it and said something to another soldier, who then turned to Opa and told him in very broken German that they needed the wagons and the horses and we must step aside so he could steer them away from us. Opa didn't understand him at first and we just kept standing there, when suddenly the soldier pushed us aside and jumped on, took the reins and drove off. Another soldier did the same with the wagon of the other people.

We just stood there, dumbfounded and speechless, until Opa started to protest. He said to the nicer soldier who let me have my doll back, "You can't do that, how can we make it back if you take the horses and the wagons? It's all we have left. You can see, we have a child with us and the other family has a baby. Don't do this to us."

His arguing could have cost us our lives, but I guess he just couldn't let them take all of the little we had left without saying something. Anyway, Opa was stopped at once when other soldiers who were suddenly standing behind him pointed their guns towards him and threatened Opa that they would shoot all of us if he didn't shut up. We were all quiet at once. One soldier waved us on so that we would move and so we did.

We made it to a little forest and stopped to catch our breath and to more or less think about which direction we should take. My mother suggested that we stay overnight because it would be a little warmer there than walking on the road, but Opa said, "We must go on. We must walk or we will freeze to death."

And so we walked in the shadow of the forest until we reached an open field. It was dark by now, but the moon gave us enough light and we realized that we were at the edge of another battlefield. Everything was still here, alarmingly still, and as we walked under the cover of the forest, we saw dead German soldiers lying all over the place, some of their bodies covered in blood, some just lying there as if they were sleeping. In all that stillness, I started to cry again because I was terrified and had to go to the bathroom. I was so scared to go away from our group, but I didn't want to pee in front of everybody. My mother hushed me and whispered that I should go behind the cover of her coat, which she had opened for me with much pain because her hands were stiff and probably covered with frostbite. She had to help me pull my underpants up again and then she whispered, "Somebody is coming towards us!"

We saw him moving but couldn't make out if he was a Russian or a German, so we went back into the forest and into the shade of the trees. Fortunately the person, whoever he was, didn't notice us. We all stood there as if we were hypnotized. We didn't move and watched him as he went from one soldier to the next, all lying on the ground, sometimes lifting their heads by their hair and shooting everybody who still showed some sign of life. He took his time to do his job. His coat was wide open as if he was sweating. He even talked to some of them. It was so awful to watch because we realized that many were still alive, but it didn't seem to concern him at all.

My mother stood beside me and suddenly she took me close to her and cuddled me right into her coat. She must have realized that I was shaking and that I wanted to run or scream, which would have given us all away. She kind of rocked me back and forth and I felt safe. We were all shaking by now and wanted to run but we had to stay still and watch this terrible act, and as he came closer, we could see him but he didn't see us. He was a Russian officer who probably made sure that nobody was alive before he, and maybe others, moved on.

I remember the killing so well, as if it just happened yesterday. The one time it was worse because we heard a whimper or a faint voice. Or was it a prayer? Anyway, when the Russian came close, he lifted this person's head and said something to him. And then he shot. It was so close, we could feel it. It was all plain killing but we couldn't do anything but watch, watch in horror as he lifted the soldier's head, let it fall to the ground and shot him in the neck. My mother whispered, "Oh God, where are you!"

By now I was so scared that I couldn't stop shivering and even though I had just gone a while ago, I peed my pants again. I couldn't control myself anymore and expected that my mother would be mad at me, but she wasn't; she put her arms tighter around me and tried to comfort me, but it didn't work. I started to sob and she held my mouth shut because any noise would have given us away. We had to watch this man for a long while and had no choice but to keep still. A bit later we heard commandos and more soldiers came.

They all pointed their guns to the ground and talked in a language still so strange to us. All of them looked rowdy and we thought for sure they would come toward us but after a moment or two the one who did the final killing gave a command and they all disappeared.

It took quite a while before we recovered from our shock and were able to start walking again. We stayed in the shadow of the forest. Opa complained that he couldn't breathe again and the baby started to cry and had to be fed. I had wet pants, but didn't complain because I was ashamed. Frau Mueller gave Opa some medicine. He was sitting in the snow, leaning against a tree. He was weak but said that we had to go on soon. "We have to cross that field we just came from to keep in the right direction, so as soon the baby is fed we have to go."

I protested. I didn't want to cross this terrible field, but both Frau Mueller and my mother told me to be quiet and to listen. I knew Opa understood my fear but he said, "We have no other choice and the sooner we leave the better." We waited until the baby was fed and was quiet again.

Frau Mueller whispered almost to herself that somehow she was glad that Renate didn't have to go through all this. "I miss her so much," she continued, "but oh God, what a sad, sad time we have to live through. I think she is in a better world now." And then she cried and my mother took her in her arms and gave her some comfort.

When we marched on, it was snowing heavily and the sky was dark. We hurried across in horror, at times not knowing what we stepped on or what we would encounter next. We stayed at the edge of the forest, always ready to hide and prepared for the worst. An hour later we made it to the other side and saw a house not too far away from us. Opa told us to stop and said, "We should see if we can stay there and have a short rest. Maybe we could at least stay long enough for the baby to be changed." (He thought about everything and we were so fortunate to have him.) We hesitated because we didn't know if the house was still occupied or maybe even taken over by Russians but when we were close enough we realized that somebody had actually opened the door a bit, and when we stood right in front of the entrance door, a woman stepped out and looked at us. She must have been middle-aged and looked as scared as we were. Opa wanted to explain but she just waved us in and told us to sit down.

We didn't know how tired we were until we sat down and she gave us a hot drink. All we wanted at this point was go to sleep, but the woman told us that we had to carry on, that we couldn't stay. She explained that the Russians had already been through her house twice and would come back again. She started to cry and said something I didn't understand and when I asked what the word "rape" meant, nobody answered. Anyway, after an hour or so we left again. My pants were almost dry, the baby was fed and changed, and we all felt a bit better again.

The woman still had tears in her eyes when we thanked her and said, "I wish I could have done more for you, but I know it is better for you to go on. I hope and pray that you will make it and will arrive back safely." She gave Opa directions, and going by that, we were on the right track and should be back home by midnight or so.

Even though we had had the rest and something warm in our bellies, we were all exhausted. Opa was still not feeling well and the baby cried constantly. But we had to go on or we would freeze to death and all of us knew that, and so we didn't complain much.

As we walked, we heard a noise again. It sounded as if a horse and a wagon were coming our way. We couldn't hide quickly enough so we had no other choice but to stop. We were scared that Russian soldiers had caught up with us again but what could we do? We stood still on the side of the road and hoped for the best.

The noise came closer quickly and then we saw two horses with a wagon coming towards us. Opa recognized the driver. It was a neighbour's servant and Opa walked right to the middle of the road to stop him. The driver, when he recognized us, looked as surprised as we were. Opa talked to him a bit in Polish and went on in German, asking him if we could get a ride back home with him. The man was not at all friendly towards Opa. He mumbled, "You know, I am not a servant anymore. I am free, free from the Germans, at last!" And he went on, now angry and louder, "Two nights ago the Russians came and liberated all of us. They freed us from you! You Germans, who forced us to work for you! You made us your slaves! But you will pay for it and all of you will be punished." He was now so enraged that we actually became scared of him. But then he calmed down a little and he looked at the woman with the crying baby and at me and said, "Fine, I will give you a ride to the house you used to live in. But I warn you, it is not your house anymore. A lot has changed since the day you left."

Opa and Frau Mueller wanted to ask him about the changes, but he just said, "Hop in or stay, I could care less, but be quick, I am getting cold." He looked at us as if we were scum and so we climbed up before he could change his mind. Opa and the other man helped us, the mother with the baby first and then the rest of us. We tried to do it on our own, but Frau Mueller had a hard time, her hands were too cold to hold on and she almost fell down again. She screamed but the man from the other family caught her and held on to her and she finally made it. We all settled down and with a big pull the horses drove on. They were too fast at first and the wagon swayed and we all fell to one side but the driver managed to straighten it out again, and after we calmed down, we were glad that we didn't have to walk anymore. Opa took a seat beside the servant but they didn't talk at all. I guess both were enemies now and we had to be thankful that we got this ride at all. We huddled together not knowing again what would happen to us next.

Much later, when it was dark, we finally arrived. We stood in front of the house and Opa and Frau Mueller had tears in their eyes. The store was closed, of course, and there was no light anywhere. The fellow who brought us back told us to wait and then he disappeared. He came back with Frau Mueller's former housemaid, who looked at us as if we came from the moon. But then she kind of smiled and asked us to come in. She pointed to the other family and asked Frau Mueller who these people were and after a short explanation she opened the door for them as well.

She didn't let us go to the front room saying, "You have to stay in what was my room," and she showed the other family to an empty room right under the roof which actually was for storage and was filled with old stuff. Opa wanted to protest but she told him that the house was partially occupied by Russians and we'd better be quiet or else. She was quite snippy now and said to Opa, "If you don't like it, you have to move on. I am actually doing you a favour in letting you stay here. I am doing you a favour because you were always good to me and my family; however, there is now no place for Germans here anymore. Remember, the sides have changed and I have to be careful that they don't find out about you and that I am helping you. We all were told by the Russians to report any German we see. We are not even allowed to talk to you anymore. So be glad that you can at least stay overnight." She pointed to the baby and said, "Make sure it doesn't cry."

She left us and Frau Mueller started to cry, but Opa hushed her and went with the other family upstairs to show them their room. We stayed in the little room where we were asked to stay. A while later Opa came back and told us not to make any noise because he heard voices coming from the main floor, probably Russians.

We were all hungry and still very cold, but we settled

on the floor, except Opa. Frau Mueller told her father to lie down on the bed because he was not feeling well at all. He protested, but she said, "Your bones are older than ours." Again he didn't want to hear what she told him, but his daughter didn't budge and to make him agree, suggested that we would take turns. He stopped arguing but insisted that at least I should sleep beside him because there was still a bit of space, "just enough for the child."

He moved right to the very edge of the bed so both of us were somewhat comfortable.

The room was small and the bed stood against one wall and was actually hidden behind a curtain to give it some privacy. Obviously, the room was meant for one person and was somewhat cozy, however now with all of us in it, it was crowded and even though the curtain was drawn open it was hard to move around. But we didn't complain; we were happy that we were not outside in the bitter cold anymore.

After we took some of our layers of clothes off and my mother and Frau Mueller found some pillows, we tried to sleep. We were so tired, but sleep wouldn't come. The voices below us became louder and it sounded as if everybody was drunk down there and was having a good time.

I think I must have fallen asleep after all because suddenly our door was thrown open and I didn't know for a moment where I was. I wanted to say something, but I felt Opa's hand on my mouth and knew that I had to be still. The door closed again and we almost thought we were safe when the door opened again and the light went on.

We saw a Russian soldier standing in the door frame. He was drunk and looked somewhat dumbfounded as if he couldn't believe what he saw and then he yelled down to the others and started laughing and yelled something down again. We all stood up, scared and afraid of what he would do to us because he reached for his gun, which was loosely hanging around his waist.

He talked to my mother, who, of course, didn't understand a word and then he pointed to Opa and pulled him and me away from the bed and pointed to my mother to lie down on it. She didn't understand what he wanted from her until he pulled her by her hair and threw her down. He ripped her clothes off and was onto her when I started to scream, saying, "Let go of my mother," but Opa pulled me back and held me close to him. Frau Mueller wanted to run out of the room, but just when she reached the door, three other soldiers showed up and dragged her back.

Opa also tried to leave the room with me, but one Russian soldier stopped him and told him to stay. Opa pointed to me and wanted to make him understand that I should not see what they planned to do with my mother and Frau Mueller, but the soldier pointed his gun to both of us and we stayed. I was terrified and Opa was completely in shock and ashamed of what I had to witness. He turned us both around so I wouldn't to be able to see, but again the soldier insisted that we watch.

They raped both women and Opa said later, that he saw approximately twenty-seven different soldiers coming and going, and coming back again.

All were so drunk and one even fell asleep right beside my mother and was pushed aside by his comrades without hesitation.

It was all over when we heard a harsh voice coming from the still wide-open door. At first nobody gave a hoot because they were too drunk to notice until a bullet went flying into the ceiling. It seemed that instantly everyone was sober and wanted to run but were stopped by this tall man, obviously their officer or commander. It seemed they were all in big trouble and would have to pay for what they had done to my mother and Frau Mueller. The officer talked to them with an icy tone and even though we couldn't understand what he was talking about, we realized that he was not pleased and they were in big trouble.

As we heard later, troop behavior depended on the disposition of the respective commander. Most officers silently tolerated the atrocities their men committed but obviously not this one. After they left, both my mother and Frau Mueller cried bitterly. They were both full of blood and bruised all over and all they wanted was to clean up because they felt dirty, degraded, and ashamed. Opa took his daughter and my mother in his arms and tried his best to comfort them, but was unsuccessful.

I didn't really know what took place, but I realized that something very, very bad had happened. Opa tried to protect me from having to watch the suffering these two had to go through, but I guess he was not very good at it. It was so sad to watch them in their agony and we all cried now and realized that this could be just the beginning of what we had to face.

The women were not able to take a bath or even clean up and by now we all stank. It was not until the next morning that the Russian officer returned and apologized for what had happened the night before. He spoke German almost perfectly and seemed to be sorry and worried. He promised that we would be safe as long we stayed in this house. He arranged that we all had a bath and that we could visit the other family upstairs. As he explained, the day before he was not aware of our presence, otherwise this all would not have happened.

We believed him and enjoyed the bath and fresh clothes we were able to get from the things we had left behind before we went on our unsuccessful escape from the Russians.

After we changed, my mother and Frau Mueller washed all the clothes we had worn and hung them up in our room to dry, which made the room even smaller.

We visited the family upstairs and realized that the baby and his mother had started to get sick, and we heard that the officer had come and had brought with him a Russian doctor who insisted that they be admitted to the town's only hospital. The husband had to stay behind and was told to move down into our room as well.

Two days later we had a knock at the door and two Polish soldiers stepped into our room.

They looked around and then told my mother and Frau Mueller to come with them. My mother wanted to know what for and was told that they needed them to clean up some facilities.

My mother was not comfortable leaving me and wanted to take me with her but the soldiers told her to leave me with Opa and the man who just moved from upstairs. They promised that my mother and Frau Mueller would return as soon as they finished the job.

Two days later, after we were worried sick, they came back. They told us that they, with many other German women, had had to clean the cells of the town's jail. It was a hard job, but they were fed well and could even take showers.

We were taken to jail

We were glad that we were together again but our relief was not long-lived because the next day, very early in the morning, we were brought to the jail that my mother, Frau Mueller, and so many other women had had to clean.

They separated us from Opa and the other man, who were put into a cell across from ours. We all cried and begged to stay together but they just pushed us in and locked the door after us. It was a fairly large cell for approximately twenty people with a small window close to the ceiling covered with iron rods that kept it dark even though the sun was shining that morning. We looked around and realized that there were already several women and children present, some of the women known to my mother and Frau Mueller because they too had cleaned the cells in this prison. They spoke a few words to each other and then we looked for a place to sit down. There were no beds or anything else to sit on, so we sat on the floor with our backs resting against the wall. The floor was covered with fresh straw and we knew that this was where we had to stay, hopefully not for long. In one corner were a few pails and we were told by the others that these were our toilets, for now anyway.

I hung onto my mother and she put her arms around me and told me that we had to be brave now.

As the day progressed, the cell filled up quickly with more and more women and children. The last were brought in late at night. They hardly found space anymore and we all had to squeeze together so they didn't have to stand up. People who were in the middle of the room sat back to back because it made it a bit more comfortable to sit for a longer time on the floor.

Frau Mueller, who was sitting beside us, whispered to Mutti, "How many more people do they want to stuff into this cell?" And my mother just said, "*Ja*, really." And she continued, "I wonder if these pails are the only place we can go to the bathroom, because I have to go and I know it will not work for me to do it in public." Frau Mueller kind of laughed and said, "Rosi, I would like to have your worries."

The one light we had was so dim that we could hardly see across the cell but this turned out to be good because we learned later that it was always left on and most of us couldn't and didn't sleep that night anyway. And many more women and children continued to come.

The place was now so full that we couldn't stretch our legs anymore and sleeping was almost impossible, even if one tried. It was all right for the first night, but later it was a pain. People who had a place against the walls were standing up so the others could sit. Everyone was stiff from sitting, and standing up and stretching was good.

We heard the cries and whispers and other noises one would only hear in private, but we learned soon that all known rules did not exist here anymore.

At six o'clock the next morning the door flew open and

we were all given a little tin container and a spoon. We were told to hold onto these utensils because if we were to lose them, we would get no food. So right away these utensils became our only, but very precious, possession.

After everybody had their utensils, breakfast came. Two men carried these big containers filled with something warm. We were told to form a line and each of us received a thin slice of dark bread and one ladle of so-called soup, which was more water than grits. It looked awful and tasted awful and I didn't want to eat it, but my mother made me by saying, "You better eat it, who knows when we will get food again. At least it is warm." (Our cell was freezing cold and we were given only one blanket for the two of us.)

Some women wanted to talk to the men who gave us our rations as they were prisoners also, but they were told right away to shut their mouth or else.

Soon after breakfast a group of women were ordered to clean the pails, which were by now full and terribly smelly. Some objected to doing such a job, but after they were hit with a rifle, everybody understood and there was no complaining about anything anymore.

They took the pails and were guided out, apparently to the courtyard, where the pails were emptied into a big hole. After that they had to rinse and clean them to be returned to the cell. When they came back, they asked if they could wash their hands. The guard just laughed and told them to sit down. It was gross!

During the day more people came and by now we were so cramped that we had to take turns sitting down. Lying down was impossible.

Two very young women were pregnant and could

hardly move around and it was hard for them to sit on the floor or later get up again. They asked the Polish guard if they could have a chair or something to sit up a bit higher than directly on the floor, but as an answer one was kicked right in the stomach. She screamed and held onto her stomach and then passed out. The other woman wanted to help her but she was threatened that she too would be punished if she didn't sit on the floor like everybody else and shut her mouth at once. She sat down but she was not able to stop her tears running down her cheeks and the guard gave her his dirty hanky and told her to stop crying.

He then went out as if nothing had happened and everybody was shocked by what had just taken place. We all realized that we were trapped and nobody would come to help us. We all were on our own and yet we somehow had to stick together.

My mother got up from where we were sitting and had a look at the young woman who got kicked. She was conscious by now and started to cry. My mother stroked her hair out of her face and offered her some water. She lifted the woman's head a bit and gave her a sip and then asked her to try to get up. My mother was so gentle with her and asked her in a low voice if she was in pain. The woman touched her big belly and shook her head and answered that she thought she was fine. With the help of another woman, my mother helped her to get to her feet and sat her on a high pile of straw which by now other people had gathered together for both pregnant women.

It was afternoon and we were all hungry and wondered if or when we would get some food again. Many children started to cry and it was a noisy, smelly place by now. We had some babies there as well and they should have been changed and fed, but nobody came until it was almost dark outside and we were all very cold.

We were relieved when the door opened and two German men came with the soup containers. They were different ones than the two in the morning and obviously they were not allowed to talk to us. Again we received bread, this time two slices and some kind of a carrot soup. It looked a bit better than the one we had in the morning, but it tasted awful, yet I didn't complain. I ate it. My mother looked at me and said, "Good girl!" Some women tried desperately to talk to the men who distributed the food because they wanted to know where their husbands were or, in our case, where Opa was but they didn't talk to us because they were being watched and looked afraid.

A bit later, after everybody had finished their food and sat back down or used the pails or even talked a bit, the Russian officer, who came to rescue my mother and Frau Mueller from those terrible soldiers the other night, stood in the door. He looked with his sharp eyes around the cell and looked over to us. He recognized us and even winked at me and suddenly turned around and left. I kind of liked him because he seemed kind or maybe had some understanding of the situation we were all in, women and children kept in jail without being guilty of a crime.

My mother said to Frau Mueller, "I wonder what he was looking for. He must be the one who is responsible for us being here. I just hope we will get out of here soon. What a stink hole we are in. I hate it!"

But Frau Mueller just said, "It could be worse."

It was bitterly cold in the cell and we were all very uncomfortable. But most of all we felt sorry for the mothers with babies and small children. It was awful to watch how they tried to calm their children, an almost impossible task.

Early the next morning a Polish nurse came in and brought some diapers with her. Somehow she knew that my mother was a Red Cross nurse and asked her to help the mothers change the babies quickly because, as she continued, "I don't have all day and have to be back soon."

My mother got up and started to help change the babies and toddlers and soon became very upset and said, "This is awful!" Most babies had sore bums so bad that they were bleeding; they needed more than fresh diapers. My mother asked the nurse if she could have water to clean them and cream to ease the pain these sores were giving them. The nurse had a look and went to the door and told the guard to open the door. The guard listened to what she had to say and shook his head. They argued but we couldn't understand what was said, but we concluded that he didn't want to allow her to get the water. Her voice became louder and more demanding and she didn't give up and a moment later the commanding officer appeared and talked to both of them. He came into the cell and walked straight to my mother. He spoke to her in perfect but funny German and my mother took him to the babies. He had one look and walked out as quickly as he could. We heard his loud commanding voice saying something to the guard and then it was quiet outside.

The nurse returned and told my mother to wait with the diapering for a few minutes because the water would come. Within a very short time two young Russian soldiers came and brought a few wash dishes and pails of warm, fresh water. The nurse brought face cloths and towels and a large container with zinc cream.

There was a lot of screaming but after about an hour all of the babies were dry and fed because bottles with milk were brought as well. The nurse turned out to be very nice and my mother was thankful that she helped us. Two women were told to collect the diapers and go with the guard to the laundry room to wash them. From then on, the babies were looked after and received fresh diapers and bottles with milk three times daily.

I think we had to thank the officer whom we knew so well by now. At least he tried to help control the agony a bit by showing some mercy and humanity.

After about three days, people started to get diarrhea and the smell became unbearable. We all looked awful and my mother said, "If we stay much longer, we will all get sick."

We heard noises and a second later screaming. At first we were not able to understand any words because of the screaming, but then we realized that these were the voices of men who were ordered to sing the German national hymn. They started to sing. At first only with low voices and only a few but then, after a big commotion and loud outcries, these men sang, all of them, loud and clear, "Deutschland Ueber Alles!" And when they were finished singing, they were hit repeatedly and were told that Germany no longer existed and therefore all Germans would be destroyed, the way they had tried to destroy the Polish people. There was a mass grave with Poles in the courtyard and that's where they would all end up. We heard the guards screaming at them, "All of you!" And after that the men cried out again because they were hit again and again and some must have fallen down because we heard the guards screaming, "Get up, get up or you die right here."

We held our breath because we realized that something very bad was happening out there.

It was awful to realize that these Polish soldiers were planning to kill all these men, maybe all of us, who knew?

The next day the same thing happened again. The men were brought into the hall, were asked to sing the German national hymn, and were beaten for singing it. We heard the whips coming down on them and then the crying out and the screams. And this was repeated until there were very few screams left. And then there was a shuffle and a slamming of a door. And then there was quiet.

We all suffered with them because we now knew the details of what was going on. The man who brought in our food gave a note to one of the women and it told us how these men, many of them husbands of women who were with us, were being punished and tortured. For many it was because the Poles and the Russians thought they were spies or it was just because they were Germans. It was awful and for us children so frightening and terrible that most of us couldn't stop shaking whenever we heard the slightest different noise outside or in the hall. We didn't understand the circumstances and why this was all happening to us.

Every day something else happened and every day was full of agony. The tension was now visible in each face, and more and more people got diarrhea and the smell was even worse. Some got so sick that they were not able to get up anymore but when the guards came in the morning, other people made sure they got up by holding them up. We were not sure anymore what they would do to us if we didn't follow their orders.

Russian soldiers raped many women almost every day. Some women were taken out of the cell and some were raped in front of everybody. It didn't matter if they were old or teenagers. The soldiers came whenever they wanted and the Polish guards just unlocked the door for them and let them do whatever they wanted.

On one occasion a soldier took an eighty-year-old grandmother with him. He went with her into a small cell, not far from ours. He was so drunk that he hardly knew where he was but he took her by her hair and when she screamed he slapped her right in the face.

Anyway, a short while later, we realized that something was burning. Our cell suddenly filled up with smoke and we started to cough and screamed for help and the women close to the door started banging against it. We were all in panic and thought for sure that this was the end because nobody opened our cell door. I thought we would be burned like the people in the windmill.

Quite a while later when we were hardly able to breathe anymore, the door was opened and two guards came in, and without any explanation we were marched out of the cell, down the stairs into the courtyard, and there we were ordered to wait. Some other guards came with the men as well. They had to wait on the other side and we were not allowed to talk but we saw their bruises and the way they stood. Many were not able to stand up straight anymore; their clothes were ripped and soiled with blood. Oh God! They looked almost as if they were dead. It was awful.

Opa was among them and I wanted to go to him and talk to him, but a guard pushed me back and showed his gun and my mother apologized for me but was told to shut up and stay in line.

Frau Mueller started to cry when she saw her father and, regardless of the guards, called over, "I love you, Papa!" The guard close to us slapped her and pushed her so that she almost fell down. My mother caught her by her arm and whispered to her to calm down or they would do more bad things to her and to Opa. She just bent her head and cried some more. It was all so very sad.

About an hour later—we were all freezing and shivering by now—the Russian officer whom we knew came and told us that there was a fire in the cell beside us, and the soldier and the woman who were in there lost their lives. Everything was fine now and we would all be brought back to our cell. There was no sorrow in his voice, it was said in a matter-of-fact tone and there was no word about why this drunken man (my mother called him a piece of shit) was with the old woman.

My mother whispered to Frau Mueller, "All he needs to say now is that he is sorry for the inconvenience." Frau Mueller didn't reply because she was still in shock about her father.

The next day we received a note again from the guy who brought our food telling us that the Russian was so drunk that he lost his cigarette and it fell into the straw, which created the smoke. Since it just smouldered and didn't burn, they did not open the door to rescue the two. Apparently many Poles hated the Russians even though they freed them from the Germans. The old woman died with the soldier; they both suffocated from the smoke.

When we returned, we realized how smelly our cell was; it stank so badly that we felt like vomiting. We could not get water to wash ourselves, only a cup of drinking water with the meals, two times a day. After about two weeks, our main job was to hunt lice, which infested our hair and our clothes. Of course fleas were also everywhere and so we were busy hunting. I had bites all over and started to get a rash and a little while later the frostbite above my toes started to get infected. After looking closely, my mother picked lice out of these sores and since we had no water to clean the wounds out, she used our drinking water. (I still have the scars.)

She reported my dilemma to the guard and surprisingly was heard. The next day a doctor came to see me and ordered that I get a bath and gave her a salve and bandages for my sores.

The "bath" was actually just a sponge bath, and I was embarrassed to take my clothes off in front of all of these people. But my mother told me that I shouldn't be silly. She was glad that we received the small dish with fresh, warm water and a bit of soap, so she got on with the job. She sponged me down and after she was finished with me, she used the water for herself and when she was done, Frau Mueller asked her if she could use it as well. My mother passed the water on to her and when Frau Mueller was ready to dump it, other people took the dish and cleaned themselves a bit as well. Before the water finally ended up in the container we used as toilets, it was dark brown. But you know, some of us felt better.

One morning we heard noises coming from the men's cell again. The screams were so loud that we screeched without making a noise. Their cell door was thrown open and we held our breath. We heard the whip going down on somebody and then the shuffle and screams again and then the shuffle and running down the stairs. We heard a door open again and after that, noises and orders came from the courtyard.

Very quickly some of the younger women built a ladder by stepping onto each other's shoulders; the last person was a boy, maybe not older than ten. At first he couldn't see much but after a few seconds he yelled out loud and said there were three men and two guards. "The men just got shovels and are digging a big hole. They are, I think, crying but the guards are pointing rifles at them. It looks like a big grave," he screamed.

Everybody was on their feet, many crying now and holding onto one another. Frau Mueller said to Mutti, "I hope they don't do anything to my father, it would kill me too."

The girl who held the boy up on top started to get tired and he had to come down. They exchanged the young woman with another and the boy climbed on top again. Just as he was about to continue with his report of what was happening in the courtyard, the door flew open and two guards stood in the doorway. They looked around and went straight to the window. The boy more or less flew down and the women jumped down as quickly as they could too. One guard took the boy by his hair and shook and slapped him until he had hair in his hand and the boy was bleeding something awful. His mother came forward to rescue him, but she too got slapped and was told to sit down or else. Then another woman stood up and demanded with a loud voice to know where her husband was. Slowly the other guard walked up to her and asked in almost a whisper, "You want to know where your husband is, ha? Well," he said, "I don't know, maybe he is still alive and is begging that he be allowed to die, or he is dead and the three men who are digging the grave will throw him in there." He grinned at first and then came close to her face and said very calmly, "Don't you worry, if he is still alive, it will not be for long. They will all be killed, if not today, then for sure tomorrow." And then he turned and spoke to all of us, "Down there where you saw the men digging, sixty Polish men are buried. They were tortured to death by the Germans before they were allowed to die. So you dare to question me where your husbands are?" And he turned and left. The other guard followed him, but before they were out of the door one turned slightly and said, "In an hour or so you can have fun again with the Russians, they are waiting already." Everybody knew what that meant.

For about one week we heard the screams and later the shots. The women never wanted to look through the window again. And after a few days, the boy had the same trouble I had, lice nested in the wound where the guard had ripped his hair out. His mother didn't ask for water; she was afraid they would do something awful to him. By the way, I never received a dish with water again. If my mother hadn't used our drink water to clean the wound, I probably would have suffered much more.

By now we were about a month in jail and many of us started to get sick. Colds and coughs were all around us but nobody cared; we all were in the same predicament. Sometimes a doctor would come, but whatever he ordered was disregarded by the guards. People were dying and nobody seemed to care.

My mother's leg was swollen and started to open up again and I knew she was in pain. The bandages she had were dirty and she too needed help. I felt sorry for her, sorry that I was not able to do anything, not for her, nor for anybody else. We were all helpless. However, one good thing came out of all of this, my mother was much nicer to me now and I almost felt secure with her. I even started to trust her.

My feet became worse too; I now had more boils above my toes and I could hardly get my booties on. But I didn't complain because so many people had worse problems. My mother said that I was brave and that she was proud of me. I glowed from her praise.

One night one of the pregnant women started to whimper and my mother got up to see if she could help her because the two pregnant women were quite often very uncomfortable lying on the hard floor. They should have had new straw; we all should have had new straw because the old straw was soiled and almost flat by now. Anyway I woke up too and wanted to go with her, but she gave me a sign to be quiet. I heard them whispering and a bit later the woman screamed, saying, "The baby is coming!" And again, "The baby is coming!"

By now everybody was awake and my mother stood up and told everyone to calm down. She made it to the door and knocked at it to get the attention of a guard. The door was opened and my mother was asked what the commotion was all about, and when my mother explained, the guard told her that he would try to get the doctor but it would take a while since he lived in town.

After about an hour or so, the doctor came. He looked at the woman and said that everything looked fine and that my mother could continue to help her, he would be back when it was time for the delivery. A little while later the door opened again and a Russian soldier came into the cell. He was drunk and the guard told us that he wanted a woman and asked who would like to volunteer. Of course everybody was quiet and tried to cover their faces, until the pregnant women started to scream again. The soldier looked up and in his drunken silliness made his way to her. He almost fell onto her and wanted to do whatever he planned to do right there, with this girl who was just ready to give birth. And because of all this commotion, the Polish guard came after the Russian and wanted to grab him away from the woman. However, in that moment we heard a shot that went into the ceiling and a second later we realized that our officer was in the cell and was pointing the gun towards both the Russian and the Pole. He said something we were not able to understand, but both made a quick turn towards the door and all three of them marched out. Shortly after that, the doctor came back to have a look again. My mother was still with the young woman and told him what had just happened. Apparently he understood German but had problems with speaking it so he didn't say much in reply to what my mother told him, but he made sure that everything was clean around the place where the baby was to be born. With the help of my mother he delivered the little baby boy. After the woman got settled again and the baby was wrapped in a blanket, the doctor told my mother that he would see to it that mother and baby would be brought over to the hospital. And so they were but we never heard from them again.

Almost two or more months later, shortly after breakfast, two strange guards came into our cell and called up some names. The women who were called were told to come forward and stand in line. My mother and Frau Mueller were among them. After they had called twelve or so together, one of the guards told us, the kids, that we didn't have to be afraid because these women would be picked up in about five minutes or so to go to work. Everyone else who was not called would stay. I remember that in seconds most women were crying because they realized that they would be separated from their children and since we all didn't trust the guards, we were afraid that we would not see each other anymore. But crying didn't help because the door opened again and the group was marched out and we were locked in again. At first everybody was quiet until many children started to cry or even scream. I was one of the older ones and felt I had to help the little ones. And so I did. I became busy and actually had fun. The remaining grown-ups were thankful since they were busy with the real small ones and so the day went by and was not too bad until it was late in the afternoon when everybody realized that the mothers wouldn't come back, not this night anyway. I started to get scared now too but didn't complain. I was too big for crying; I was, after all, almost grown up now. At least that's how I felt.

We were alone for about four days when the door was opened and the twelve women came back. They looked worn out and tired but we didn't mind; we had our mothers back and were not alone anymore.

Later, they told us that they had had to close trenches that the Germans had built close to the town. It was a brutal job; they shoveled the wet, muddy, and most of the time still-frozen dirt down into the trenches. They showed us their hands and feet, which were full of blisters and sores. The only thing good about it was that the food was not too bad and they were fed three times a day. They even had a shower before they returned. We were surprised and asked right away where they had had a shower. Well, they told us, they stayed in a camp during the nights and that's where the showers were. They were told that the camp was a concentration camp, previously occupied by Jewish and Polish prisoners who were just liberated by the Russians a short while ago. My mother said it looked awful inside, worse than here.

A week or so later, we heard from the cell across from us the now so familiar noises: the terrible screams and then a few gun shots. And as always, most of us started to shiver, some couldn't stop the chatter of their teeth, and others, without control, peed their pants.

After a moment's silence, we heard the footsteps coming and then commands and shuffling as if people were carrying something down the stairs. We heard the doors being thrown open and after that, commotion from the courtyard. Quickly, as before, the women built the human ladder up to the window. The boy on top was again to report what he saw and what was going on down there. He was very quiet at first but then reported that some prisoners were burying other prisoners. However, he was not able to recognize who they were. He said that the guards were screaming at them and making signs to hurry up. This was the mass grave the Polish guards told us about earlier. They claimed that during the German occupation, many Polish prisoners were buried there. And now they did the same with us, the Germans.

Our cell was by now so filthy that we couldn't stand it anymore. Some of us complained and were told that we would get out of there soon. And so it was. Just a day or so later, all of the women and children were loaded onto Russian army trucks. It was a cold morning and all of us were scared and didn't know what would happen to us next. The Russian soldiers who picked us up did not have much patience and waved us on to hurry up with getting on the trucks. These trucks were open and without protection and in no time we were freezing. A guard from the jail came towards us and some women asked him if he could tell us where we were going but he didn't answer and just pointed to hurry up. After about twenty minutes or so, all of the women and children from our cell were loaded and the women were sitting against the walls of the trucks and we children were put in the middle. It was tight but it kept us warmer. The soldiers jumped up, too, and pushed so that they could sit down as well. They looked mean and held their rifles right in front of them. Minutes later we were on our way to another unknown destination. Frau Mueller wondered where her father would end up but as soon the Russian soldier saw her speaking to my mother, he told her to shut up.

The concentration camp

AT FIRST WE SAW ONLY A BIG COMPLEX AND MY MOTHER SAID that this was the place where they had had their shower. The complex was surrounded by a high wire fence and a gate that was patrolled by Russian soldiers. They, too, had guns and rifles but had them loosely hanging over their shoulders. They looked tired and uninterested. However, they stopped the trucks and showed the drivers which direction they should take. The place looked dead. We saw deserted barracks, actually rows of them, but it was scary quiet. The trucks stopped in front of one of the barracks and we were ordered to get off and stand in line. At first nobody spoke to us. We got colder by the minute; it was very early on a cold March day.

Suddenly all of the soldiers stood at attention and then we saw "our" officer again. He spoke first to his soldiers and then turned towards us saying that we had arrived at the former concentration camp where Jews, mostly Poles, were kept by the Germans. He continued in saying that this would be, until further notice, our new home and that we should make the best of it. He added, more to himself, that at least this camp had no gas chambers. We didn't understand what he meant and just looked emptily up at him. He told us that he expected us to work and to obey orders. Severe punishment would be given to those who thought this was a vacation property. "Remember, you are Germans and many, many people suffered under your government and some of the guards here might take revenge. I will try to make sure that you are treated fairly but I will not always be here to control it, so blend in and behave."

After he left we were told that before we could get to our quarters, we would first get something for the lice and fleas everybody had by now. Of course at first we thought this was great, until they came with DDT powder. They sprayed this poisonous powder with large syringes right into the collar of our clothes, first the front, then the back. It was a terrible feeling and the smell was so bad that I had to throw up from it. They said that within a short while the pests we had would disappear. And so they did, except that many of us got a skin rash later on. I thought this was worse than the lice and fleas because at least you could catch these little buggers once in a while. And the sores we had started to sting from the powder and the pain didn't go away. The frostbite on my feet became bad again and my mother's leg opened up and the ulcer was now worse than before. We needed bandages and medication but we had none. We needed a doctor, but had only three or four nurses and they were too busy caring for much more acute cases. We were told that at least we didn't have bugs anymore, so we should be glad of that.

After we were sprayed, we were guided into one of the barracks. It smelled awful inside but it was still better than the cell we were in before. At least here we each got a bed with fresh straw and a blanket on top. And another nice thing was that we could go to an outhouse, not like in the jail cell, where we only had pails. I thought this was all pretty fantastic and felt so much better. Even the doors were open, and we children could go outside and play.

Early the next day some women had to return to the jail we had just come from to clean the cells. I am sure the dirt we left behind was not pretty. Again, we kids were separated from our mothers for a while. But this time it was just for a day or two and, since we were familiar with the procedure by now, we were not too worried anymore.

The women came back the next night but many were depressed and crying. Apparently most of the women had been raped and were terribly treated. Many had bruises and a few had their hair shorn and looked like ghosts, and worse, my mother told Frau Mueller, they were so scared that they could be infected with syphilis because apparently many soldiers had that sickness and it was contagious. By now I understood what rape was. I knew this was what the soldiers had done to my mother and Frau Mueller the first night after we had to return to Szubin. However, what was syphilis? I had no clue and when I asked my mother, she just said, "You wouldn't understand, but it is a bad disease and there is no cure for it if you don't have the proper antibiotics."

My mother was scared, too; even though she had not been raped this time she was thinking back to the time when she and Frau Mueller were raped. And so they were in the same predicament as all the others. There was no knowing if they were all infected. When a female warden came in, my mother asked her if there was something that could be done now rather than later to prevent an infection. But she was told that she as a nurse should know better than to ask. "There is no cure once you are infected.

The only thing which would help is penicillin and this medication is not available at all. Not for Germans, that is for sure. But I tell you what, I will allow you all to have a shower, at least that would make you feel better."

And so our life in prison continued, not in a jail anymore, but in the same camp in which many Polish Jews and politically incorrect Germans had lost their lives during the occupation of the German regime. They were not killed by gas here, but died because they were treated like rats, or so we were told.

Our mornings started with getting up and going outside, standing in rows and saying "here" when our name was called. Small children were carried in their mothers' arms and the older children had to stand in front of their mothers.

Sometimes we were allowed to shower but most of the times we didn't wash at all.

After a meager breakfast the women were picked up for work. There were still many trenches to be closed and regardless of how weak some were, they had to do the jobs they were told to.

The men, who were in barracks across from us, had to work as well. What they had to do, we didn't know. The compound was separated so that we hardly knew what was going on over there. All we realized was that everyday more and more came; some were marched in and some came by truck as we had. Some were dressed in what was once a suit, some in uniforms, but all looked awful and defeated.

Most of the barracks were filled up by now. Every day more women and children came and two weeks later small children had to sleep with their mother in one bunk bed. But still, it was better than in the jail cell where we couldn't even stretch out and had to sit on the floor most of the time.

About two weeks after we were brought here, "our" officer, accompanied by a man in civilian clothes and a soldier, came in. They looked around and walked right up to my mother. The officer introduced my mother to a man called Mr. Anaszevich. Apparently he was the real owner of the dispensary and drugstore where we had lived until the Russians liberated Poland and from which we fled with Frau Mueller and her father. Mr. Anaszevich looked at my mother with friendly eyes and said something in Polish to the officer. They talked for a few moments and then the man turned back to my mother and in broken German he asked her if she would be interested in working for him. He explained that he had returned from a German concentration camp a few weeks ago and had moved back into his house, which had been confiscated by the Germans before he, his wife, and his mother-in-law were put into camp. He heard that his wife and mother-in-law were alive and would return a bit later but in the meantime he needed help. My mother didn't understand at first and asked why her, since Frau Mueller lived in the house before and was probably more qualified to do the job, but he answered that he wanted her and she should make up her mind. He said that he heard that she was a Red Cross nurse and, therefore, would qualify for the job just fine. Of course my mother said yes, but her next question was what would happen to me. He answered that I had to stay in the camp, "But you will always return at night anyway." The officer confirmed, "Nothing will happen to your little daughter."

Back to the house we just left a while ago

AND SO IT WENT FOR ABOUT FOUR WEEKS; SHE WOULD LEAVE early in the morning and would return at about five o'clock in the afternoon. She told Frau Mueller that he was a gentleman through and through and even paid her a few zlotys, which was the Polish currency.

The arrangement was good for us and actually later for many of us because Mr. Anaszevich was wonderful, very understanding and generous. A tall, interesting man, he was skinny rather than slim and his hair was snow white. He wore a little mustache and had such very sad, blue eyes. And the most surprising thing was that he treated my mother with respect. He was a gentleman.

He understood what my mother was going through because he had just come out of the hell she and all the others in camp were in now. And when one day he realized that she was stealing medication for her fellow inmates, he told her that it would be better to ask him first rather than steal.

Her work involved almost everything, from housework

to shoveling snow and cleaning the sidewalk, to helping him fill orders and prescriptions for his customers.

The house was like a warehouse; it was filled with groceries and other goods he would take as payment for the medicine he dispensed.

So at first the temptation to steal was there and my mother did steal until he caught her. As she later told us, she thought for sure he would call the Polish police and we all knew what that would have meant, probably death.

Anyway, one cold, snowy afternoon she stole two packages of butter that she put right into her bosom. She packed one to each side and when she felt the butter become soft she would go outside and shovel snow and so on. He must have realized that she shoveled snow quite often that day and questioned her about it. At first she blamed the weather. However, she must have looked guilty and he became suspicious. He told her to do something else and stop worrying about the snow and after a while, I guess, she had to admit that she had packed her bosom full of butter packages. There was no way out anymore since it showed pretty soon. She had to tell him what she did and that she was truly sorry. And instead of reporting her to the police, he told her that he knew for quite a while that she had been taking things. He said to her, "I do understand but please, as I told you before, never lie again. Ask me instead." He continued, saying, "I was where you are now, except when we were caught we were shot. So tell me whenever you need something, just don't lie." And from then on she never took anything without asking him. And most of the time he offered her to take what she needed, food or medicine, later even clothes. He had the whole house full of food and clothes since that was how business was conducted in those days. Money was worthless. Food, clothes, and even soap were valuable. Yet if people came to his store without having anything to exchange and needed medicine, he would give it to them without question, telling them to pay for it whenever they were able to do so.

Yes, he was a good man and we were so lucky to ever have met him. He and "our" officer were our guardian angels.

It was in mid-spring when my mother returned from her work and told me that Mr. Anaszevich asked her to bring me along because he needed somebody to rinse empty bottles.

She received a letter from him for the camp authorities and I was allowed to go with her to work. It was strange for me to go out on the street and walk with my mother again. The way to the store took about almost an hour to walk but I didn't mind even though my feet hurt. I promised to be a good girl and to always do what Mr. Anaszevich asked me to do. My mother told me that he was a very generous and understanding man, so I should not make him angry or upset him in any way. I promised.

And truly he was all that my mother said about him. As a matter of fact, the first day I did not work at all, but rather had to admire the little zoo he kept in the backyard. He walked with me for quite some time and explained every animal he had in detail to me. For instance, I learned that the zoo was more an animal hospital because whoever found or had a hurt or sick animal would bring it to him to look after it. He even had a stork and right away I asked him if it would bring a baby soon. He laughed so hard about my question that I thought at first I had said something wrong because I thought it certainly was not funny. But he told me that he wished that this stork would deliver a baby since he and his wife never had children; but no, this stork was sick and now he didn't want to fly away anymore. "I guess I spoiled him too much."

I learned to do little jobs and certainly was never too busy to ask him questions about everything and in a very short time I learned to like this man very much. As a matter of fact, we felt quite well by now working for Mr. Anaszevich.

In early summer, Mr. Anaszevich told my mother that he expected his wife and his mother-in-law to return back home within the next few days. My mother looked so upset that he realized that she thought this would mean the end of our employment. So he told her not to worry, because both were certainly not able to look after the big house and he still needed her. And of course he was sure his wife would be delighted to have me too. She loved children, he told my mother, and since I was a good kid, he was certain that his wife would approve of my staying.

The next few days before their arrival became very busy because my mother worked hard to bring everything to order. The day before they were due, the house was spotless and Mr. Anaszevich was pleased with her.

Early afternoon the next day, he picked them up from the train station and I guess seeing each other after many years was not easy for the three of them. As he told us before, both ladies were in different concentration camps and, until a few months ago, no one knew whether they were still alive or not. So the first day we didn't see much of the two ladies and only later were we introduced to his wife and his mother-in-law. I didn't like either one of them, especially the mother-in-law, who looked so strict that I got the shivers. They both spoke Polish with us and insisted that we learn the language. They told us by showing us what to do and often Mr. Anaszevich came to rescue us by translating from Polish to German what was asked of us. Well, it was hard at first, but since we didn't want to go back to the camp we tried, and in a way, we got along.

As a matter of fact, after a week or so Mr. Anaszevich came to my mother to tell her that he received permission for us to stay and live with them. Of course only if we wanted to. And boy, did we want to! So my mother thanked him and he showed us the room we could stay in. It was the room right under the roof above the old one in which we had stayed when we lived with the Muellers.

We had no washroom there but he said we could share the bathroom with a Russian officer, "He is hardly ever home and wouldn't even know. Just make sure that you don't use it when he is home and don't leave any of your belongings in there." He kind of laughed his funny laugh, the laugh I liked so much on him, and said, "You will see."

We were actually surprised that somebody else lived in the house other than the Anaszeviches. We never saw anybody during the day. So my mother agreed and promised that we would make sure that we only used the bathroom when this officer was out. How we would do it we didn't know yet, but surely there would be a way to avoid contact.

When we returned to the camp for the last time that night and told everybody about the offer, all of us were sad. Frau Mueller started to cry, understandably; not only were we close by now, but for her it was still her house.

When they bought it they didn't know that it was actually confiscated property, confiscated from a Jewish couple the Nazis sent to concentration camps. And now we would live there and she had to stay here in this lousy camp. It was not fair and my mother felt so sorry for her, but what could she do? It was an opportunity we could not let pass.

All the others said they would miss all the good things my mother often brought for them. So it was a sad time for all, except for us, of course, because we didn't have to come back. We sure wouldn't miss the camp. But we had to leave them behind and felt bad and guilty about it, yet we couldn't change anything. We were just so lucky and we knew how blessed we were.

The next morning, before we left, we were called into the warden's office. There we were told that we were under a curfew and had to be off of the streets by 6:00 pm. We were also marked with a big swastika, painted with white oil paint on both sides of our coats.

They told us that we should never forget what the Germans did to them and if we didn't follow the rules we could easily be back in the camp again.

When we arrived that morning with our few belongings, Mr. Anaszevich saw what they did to our coats. He was upset and said, "That was not necessary, but that's what the Nazis did with us so I guess some people couldn't resist doing it to you. Well, it will soon be summer and you won't have to put your coats on for quite a while." But a bit later we had to wear the swastika on all our clothes and we were punished if we didn't do so.

After we moved in, Mrs. Anaszevich called us to tell my mother what her duties would be and gave me a few small jobs as well. My mother was now officially their maid and was not to help Mr. Anaszevich at all anymore. He objected that I had jobs at all, but my mother said that this was all right; I should at least do some little things, otherwise I would be bored.

The mother-in-law was always watching us and made me quite uncomfortable. She was strict and I was afraid of her. She was a tall skinny woman with short, thin, grayish hair, combed straight back. She was always dressed in black, which made her even stricter looking. Oh yes, I was totally afraid of her and I called her a witch when I was thinking about her.

But soon I learned that she too was a kind person who wanted only the best for us. For example, one afternoon she called me down into her room where she sewed a lot and made things they needed for the house. She said to me that she had found a pair of old curtains and thought they would be enough for a dress for me. So she took my measurements and in no time I had a new dress that I even liked. I wore it without the swastika.

One day she saw me in the garden talking to the stork and when she asked me what I was telling him, I answered that I would like to have a brother or sister I could play with. She laughed and said that he would not bring me a sister or brother but what about a little dog?

Well, I found that idea fantastic and told her that I would like that. And so after about two weeks we had a little puppy, a black Scottie, which we named Blacky. At that time I didn't know what black meant, because I didn't speak English, but learned that she spoke perfect English and French and actually so did Mr. and Mrs. Anaszevich.

A few weeks after the two women had arrived they

told my mother that they had invited some people and planned to have a little dinner party. They were planning to serve a roast and wanted to have dumplings with it. They looked for a big cook pot but couldn't find one anywhere, and asked my mother if she had any idea where else to look. My mother had an idea all right but she didn't want to tell them about it. Up in the attic was such a pot, but we used it as our pee pot during the night. We sure didn't want to disturb anybody, especially not the Russian officer whom, by the way, we had still never met.

Early in the morning my mother tried to clean the pot, but because we had used it for a while and sometimes it had to wait to be cleaned, I guess it developed a certain smell. Anyway, my mother told them she had not seen a big pot but, out of precaution, she returned the pot back to its original place, in the attic. She told me, just in case they had the idea to check the attic and maybe even our room too. And so it was, a day later, my mother was asked to go with Mrs. Anaszevich to see what was kept up in the attic.

After about fifteen minutes they returned and Mrs. Anaszevich carried "our" pot down like a trophy. My mother tried so hard to talk them out of using it and came up with all sorts of excuses but without success. This was the right pot and it was to be used.

When my mother pointed out that it stank, she was told to boil it with water a few times and the smell would disappear. The mother-in-law told her it stank because it had probably been up there for a hundred years; so she should not worry, the pot was perfect.

When the day of the dinner party finally had arrived, my mother and I were desperately trying to avoid disaster but it was out of our control unless we were to tell them the truth, which of course we wouldn't or couldn't do.

We never tasted the dumplings and told them the next day, when we had leftovers, that we were not feeling well and couldn't eat.

The house smelled something awful. Even Mr. Anaszevich complained about it, but I guess the dumplings must have tasted all right, because they talked about the party and its success for days and wanted to give another party again soon.

Will we ever go back to Germany?

ONE MORNING, AFTER MY MOTHER HAD MADE SURE THAT THE officer had left, she and I went down to the bathroom. I was sitting on the throne and she was getting ready, brushing her teeth and combing her hair, when the door opened and the Russian was standing in the door frame. It was "our" officer or, as mother called him, our guardian angel. After a speechless second my mother apologized and wanted to rush out of the bathroom. He, however, made a gesture that we should stay and finish whatever we had to do. He turned around and told her in his perfect but accented German, that he would come back.

My mother was shocked that we lived under the same roof. It was amazing that we hadn't run into each other before or had he made sure that we hadn't? He must have known that we now lived here. And that was why Mr. Anaszevich laughed when he told us that a Russian officer lived in the house.

Anyway when my mother told Mr. Anaszevich about the incident, he laughed again and told her that "Mikhail" had told him about us in the first place. Mikhail had made the suggestion that my mother should help Mr. Anaszevich and later also suggested that I should come as well. So, yes, he knew that we lived in the little room above him. He didn't want us to know, because he thought my mother would be scared of him. Mr. Anaszevich heard from the officer what the soldiers had done to my mother and Frau Mueller and that he felt sorry for us. My mother asked right away if he was able to do something for Frau Mueller as well but Mr. Anaszevich shook his head saying, "No, he can't do anything for her. She and her husband were Nazis. Everybody in town knew about them. Why do you think they got my store?" My mother was shocked. She couldn't believe what she heard. So she answered that this must be a mistake because Frau Mueller was such a nice and helpful person, and, she continued, that Frau Mueller told her that they bought the store in 1940 from a Polish couple who wanted to sell because they wanted to go to America.

He smiled and said that this couple was he and his wife, but he didn't want to sell; it was taken from him and yes, they wanted to go to America, but it was too late for that. Instead, the Nazis put him, his wife, and his mother-in-law, who lived with them, in three different concentration camps. "And here we are," he continued, "alive and back in our house. I must say, I don't know how I can ever thank God enough for letting us live. So Pani Rosa (that's what he called my mother), don't talk to me about the Muellers."

My mother was so sad about what she had heard because she knew Frau Mueller and her father were not bad people, and since she had never gotten to know Mr. Mueller, she refused to believe the whole story.

After a few days I met our officer in the hall. I was scared of him because I remembered the soldiers and what they did and the shot and the crying and screaming. And so I ran down the stairs and fell. He came after me and picked me up and said, "I won't hurt you. I have a little girl like you at home. I won't hurt you." He took his handkerchief out of his pocket and wiped my tears and then my nose. He put me down, and he repeated again, "I won't hurt you, Steffie." And I believed him, but I still ran down the stairs as fast I could because now I was embarrassed.

By now it was July and we started to become very homesick. We didn't have it bad at all; sure my mother had to work hard and I had certain duties too, but the Anaszeviches treated us well. And yet, we were prisoners and had to walk around with a swastika painted on all our clothes. Yes, we wanted to go home.

We heard from others that the war was over and Germany was completely in ruins and we wondered if my stepfather was still alive. I myself thought often about my foster parents. Would I ever see them again?

I never mentioned them to my mother because I didn't want to make her mad. Mind you, she was so much better to me now; she didn't hit me anymore and she didn't have the fits she used to have if I did something wrong. However, I didn't trust her because I would never forget how she was to me when we still were at home.

Anyway, we were stuck with the Anaszeviches and had to be thankful for it because other prisoners had it much worse. Many were killed in unspoken ways.

Once in a while my mother had to go back to the camp to deliver medication and other items and when she returned she told me that she talked to some people we knew. They all said we should not complain because it was like hell in camp. The food was so bad that many people became sick and were close to dying. And the Russians still raped the women and young girls and many were killed in horrible ways. The other woman who was pregnant while we were in jail had twins, but one baby was killed right after it was born by a Russian soldier who threw it against the wall. Again, the commandant came in time and the other baby was saved. My mother was always so depressed when she returned.

On one occasion I asked her why she was so sad and she told me that she spoke to Frau Mueller. Frau Mueller was working for a Polish family as well but had to return every evening to the camp. She told my mother that it was not too bad at all. However, she didn't know where her father was. She tried to find out by asking around but was told by the wardens to shut up or else. My mother said she looked so sad when she talked about her father. Frau Mueller thought her father was dead.

After I heard the news, I was sad too. Opa was a nice man and I loved him. He was such a good person, so why would people be so mean to him? But Mutti said I shouldn't be upset, because if he died, he was now with Renate in a better world. "Just try to remember the nice times you had together," she said.

The little dog they bought for me was always around me and we had a lot of fun together. One morning when I helped Mutti clean the bedrooms, Blacky went in the mother-in-law's bedroom and started to tear a pillow apart. By the time we realized what was happening it was too late. The room was like clouds in the sky and Blacky was not black anymore, but rather snow white. Of course I thought this was great and went right into it as well. Later, I was sure my mother and the Anaszeviches would have a stroke or something, because they were all screaming, but the more they screamed the more we had fun. It was almost impossible to get us out because the down feathers became thicker by the second and after about two minutes or so, the room and the upstairs hall were full of them.

Anyway, when I finally had Blacky in my arms and came out of the bedroom, we both looked like snowmen. My mother was so, so mad and the only person who really thought this was funny was Mr. Anaszevich. He laughed so hard that he had to hold his tummy.

If I remember correctly, it took my mother almost the whole day to clean the mess and even after days we still found feathers all over the house.

At the beginning of September I was told by Mrs. Anaszevich that I had to go to school. It was a terrible thought because I didn't speak much Polish and also had no clothes without a swastika. I was not allowed to wear the dress Mrs. Anaszevich had made for me in public or they would have been in trouble. So I told her that I would not go and started to cry. But she was not able to help me because this was ordered by the government; there was nothing she could do about it.

The next morning Mr. Anaszevich brought me to the same school I had actually gone to before we fled from Szubin. They put me in Grade One because I couldn't speak the language. All of the pupils started to laugh when they saw the swastika on my dress. They called me a stupid German. I was so embarrassed and frightened that I started to cry and the more I cried, the more I was teased.

When school was over I was picked up again by Mr.

Anaszevich and the teacher told him what had happened. I didn't know what they talked about but after a while we went to the principal's office and the next day I didn't have to go back to school anymore.

My mother was not impressed by my behaviour and for the first time in a long while she screamed at me again. But Mr. Anaszevich took my side and told her he was sad that the children were mean but that it was hard for children to understand. He told my mother, "One day when Steffie speaks Polish, she will go back to school."

The next day we were asked to come down to the living room where both Mr. and Mrs. Anaszevich and the mother-in-law were waiting for us. We were asked to sit down and after a short quiet moment I became scared. Maybe they were going to ask us to go back to the camp? And if so, it was my fault because I didn't want to go to school. But soon we realized that this was not the case at all because they asked my mother if she wanted to give me up for adoption. They explained that because they had no children and they had fallen in love with me, they would give me a good home, love and education, and everything a child at my age should have. They had seen what happened to me yesterday in school and adoption would change all this. I would be sent to a private school and, of course, be without the swastika. They smiled at their suggestion but I was in shock. I didn't want to stay with them. No way. If I had to stay with anyone, then I would go back to my foster parents; but I would not stay here, not with them, far away from home. I liked them, but not as my parents.

My mother seemed puzzled as well. She looked at me and then at them and shook her head and said, "It is nice of you to think so highly of Steffie. But I cannot just give her up, not now anyway. I have to talk about it with Steffie too. She might not like the idea and I have to think about it myself. So please give us time." They understood her reaction, of course, but I didn't.

When we were in our room I started to cry and told her that I was homesick. I said, "I want to go back to Berlin. I don't want to stay here. Tell them that we need to go home and see if Papa is all right. I beg you, don't give me to them. Tell them we have to go back to Berlin. Please!"

But she said, "I have to think about it. Maybe it would be good for you." The next morning she told me that she would not give me to the Anaszeviches. And for the first time my mother mentioned that she had spoken to somebody who would help us to escape. God, this was news! However, it was even more terrible than to give me away. This meant we could be killed. I, just nine years old, told her that she should not think about escaping.

"Mutti," I said, "Tell the Anaszeviches that we both don't want to stay. All we want is to go home. We are homesick. Maybe they will help us. Tell them about the escape plans. But tell them also that we wouldn't do it because they are good to us and we will not pay them back by running away from them."

She looked at me, took me in her arms, and said, "You are right. These people are so nice to us; at least we owe them honesty. And before we do something stupid I need to explain everything to them. Maybe they will help and understand that I don't want to give you up and that we are both homesick. But, on the other hand they could call the police and then I don't know what will happen to us."

I shook my head and said, "They will not call the police. Maybe they will tell us that they can't help but they will not call the police."

So we went down to talk to them again. They asked us to come in and, like the day before, we were all sitting in their living room. My mother started at once and explained why she couldn't leave me with them. And then she also told them about the escape she had planned for us and that she met a man a few weeks ago who offered to help us, of course for a price. My mother still had her wedding ring and the few zlotys Mr. Anaszevich had given her and for this, the man had agreed to take us to the German border. But she continued, "I can't do it. After all, you are so good to us. I just can't do it." She looked at Mr. Anaszevich and said, "It would be so wrong to just go away without showing our gratitude to you, your wife, and your mother-in-law." She paused, tears rolling down her cheeks, and after a moment she continued saying, "Yes, it would be so wrong but we are so homesick." And then she asked if they could help us go back home. She blew her nose and looked so very sad and helpless.

There was a long pause during which no one said a word and you could have heard a pin drop, and then Mr. Anaszevich started to smile and said, "Pani Rosa, we know about your plans. Our Russian friend Mikhail, you know the officer who lives here and actually recommended you to us, told us." We looked at him as if he had come from the moon. We couldn't believe that they knew about our plans. But they knew. He explained that the man who wanted to help us was in jail. Apparently he had promised to help people escape and then as soon he brought them close to the German border, he shot them. Then he would take everything useful that he found on them and leave them there to rot. We probably would have been in the same predicament. It was just by accident that he was found out. And when he actually confessed, he mentioned that he was in contact with my mother as well.

My mother and I just sat there, speechless. We didn't know what to say. We were guilty and thought for sure that we would have to go back to the camp and be punished, maybe shot, who knows. My mother started to cry and then all she said was that she was sorry. And Mr. Anaszevich replied, "We know but I still cannot understand that you wanted to risk both of your lives. What were you thinking? We are glad that you finally told us about your plans and we will try to help you. I must ask Mikhail not to go further with your case. We hope he will understand. You are lucky, Pani Rosa! We will try to get proper papers for you."

Mother looked up and mumbled, "What do you mean papers? How will you get proper papers for us? We are prisoners and nobody will give us papers."

They all smiled now and Mrs. Anaszevich answered, "I will go by train to Poznan and I will try to get papers for you so you can go back to Berlin legally."

We were both so surprised about all the news that we didn't know anymore whether we should laugh or cry. But then my mother just went forward and we all hugged, laughed, and cried together. Mr. Anaszevich stroked my hair and said, "We understand and we will help you to return safely back home to Berlin. But we will be sad when you leave us. It will be quiet without Steffie, but we understand. She brought us so much joy. Oh yes, we will miss you both."

We went back to our room and my mother cried some more and every so often she said, "I don't believe it, it can't be true. They are Jews and not long ago they were prisoners themselves. And now they want to help us. I can't believe it! We were their enemies and now they want to help us to go back home. Legally! I can't believe it." And then she prayed and thanked God. And I knew we were in danger and that the Anaszeviches had saved us from being punished or even killed, and I too thanked God when praying that night.

My mother had to prepare the evening meal and we went down to the kitchen. Mrs. Anaszevich told my mother to set the table for six and we thought they were having company. After a while she said, "Change Steffie's clothes and let her put on the dress my mother made for her, and you try to change into something nicer too. Mikhail will join us too and we will celebrate your honesty and, hopefully, we can help you get the proper papers to go home to Berlin soon."

It was a warm early September evening and we were excited that we were invited for dinner. My mother helped me put on the nice dress which Pani Oma, that's what I called Mrs. Anaszevich's mother, had made for me, and my mother changed into a clean blouse but didn't have a clean skirt. She combed her hair longer than normal but looked pale and shabby. She wished she had some make-up, but of course had none.

When we entered their dining room we were not sure if it was appropriate for us to be there. But the Anaszeviches made it easy for us to overcome our shyness. Mikhail, "our" officer, who had a drink in his hand, bowed in front of us and smiled, and Mr. Anaszevich offered us a drink as well. My mother had a glass of wine and I had juice. We all looked festive, even Pani Oma, who always wore black dresses with high collars, which made her look so strict and cold. This evening she wore a dark blue dress with a not-so-high collar and a nice gold chain.

I was proud of the dress I wore. I knew I looked cute.

At first my mother was very quiet because they spoke Polish and we could hardly understand what they were talking about, until Mikhail realized that we didn't understand and started to speak some German. Slowly they had a conversation going and my mother, who had by now another glass of wine, participated a bit.

Mrs. Anaszevich went to the kitchen and of course my mother followed her. Soon dinner was served and I was glad they didn't serve dumplings. By now we were all more relaxed and the conversation was going on in Russian, Polish, and German. For me a dinner party was something new and I was so happy that I had been invited as well.

After dinner my mother cleared the table but Mrs. Anaszevich helped her, which she never did when they gave other dinner parties. There my mother would do the serving and I had to stay in the kitchen and help with everything I was able to help with.

My mother mentioned that we had better leave now but they all said that we should stay a bit longer and Mikhail asked my mother if she would play the piano for them. My mother was surprised, of course, that he knew that she could play but, although shy at first, she agreed to play if they had some music books. They had and for the first time in more than a year I heard her playing the piano again. It was beautiful and she was applauded for it.

After that they talked a bit longer but my mother, who didn't want to overstay our welcome, said that we should go now and thanked all of them for having us. And when we were on our way out Mikhail asked her if she could play one more song. She looked at the Anaszeviches and Pani Oma kind of gave her a smile and agreed in saying, "Pani Rosa, play one more song." And to Mikhail, "What would you like to hear?" Everybody was surprised when he said, "Silent Night". My mother thought at first that he was joking, but he explained, "I know it sounds funny to ask to hear a Christmas song in September, but it reminds me of home, my wife, and my little girl, who looks as cute as little Steffie."

And so my mother played "Silent Night" at the beginning of September 1945 for a Russian officer who was as homesick as we were. Tears were streaming down his cheeks and we could see that in his thoughts he was not sitting with a Polish family and their guests, a German woman and her daughter.

Embarrassed, he apologized for crying and then thanked my mother for playing for him. He said, "It was a pleasure to listen to your performance. I will not be back home with my family for Christmas but you will and I will help Mrs. Anaszevich get you the papers you need to return home. Promise me, no more stupid and dangerous actions on your part." My mother promised and thanked everybody, and we left for our little room.

A week later Mrs. Anaszevich made the train trip to Poznan. "Our" officer gave her a document that approved our release and with that he told her that she should have no problems getting the proper travel papers for us.

We will go home

In the meantime Pani Oma became busy preparing us for our trip. She made another, much warmer dress for me. It was not very pretty but very practical. She went shopping with my mother and bought new stockings for us and I had to knit socks and gloves. Of course she helped because I never would have had them ready for our trip. Oh, she was so strict, kind but strict. If she gave you an order you had better do it or you would hear about it. Mr. Anaszevich was afraid of her too. But he made sure he didn't see her too often. When we were alone he would make fun of her but told me never to tell her or she would hit him, which of course was a joke, but at that time I believed him.

One day she told my mother to bring our coats to her. My mother looked at her and asked, "What for?"

She answered, "As I remember you both have the swastika painted on your coats. You cannot travel with that; we have to try to get rid of it. Go to my son-in-law and ask him for something that will do that." My mother brought both of the coats to her and then asked Mr. Anaszevich if he could give her something to get rid of the oil paint. He gave her a bottle but said right away, "It will stink but it will also help keep the lice away should you encounter these pests on your trip again."

Well, he was right. He had given her turpentine and the smell was awful but it did a fairly good job. When we put the coats on at least we didn't look branded. Pani Oma inspected them and was satisfied. She told my mother that later a dressmaker could turn the material inside out and that would give us almost new coats. I think that is what my mother later did.

Mr. Anaszevich seemed very quiet and sad. I asked him why and he looked at me and his face became even sadder. And then he explained, "I will miss you so much, Steffie." Somehow he smiled and then continued in telling me that nobody would help him feed his animals anymore and Blacky would really miss me. And with that he made me sad too but I told him that I had to see my Papa and maybe my other Mutti and Papa. He was surprised that I had another Mutti and Papa and I tried to explain that I was not allowed to see them but maybe I could visit them when we came home. I was not sure if he believed everything I was trying to tell him but I guess he didn't understand what I was talking about and he didn't ask any further. Maybe he thought I was making up a story, which I did sometimes, but not this time.

After about three days Mrs. Anaszevich came back from her trip. She told us it was hard to get what we needed to go by train back to Germany and, if she hadn't had the letter from Mikhail, she never would have been able to get the papers and the train tickets.

My mother looked at her and said, "Train tickets?"

"You mean you have train tickets for us?" I asked too.

"Steffie," my mother said, "Did you hear? Mrs.

Anaszevich has our train tickets! Oh, how can we ever thank you!" And suddenly she took Mrs. Anaszevich in her arms and gave her a kiss and at the same time apologized for it. But Mrs. Anaszevich didn't mind at all and they both cried and laughed together.

We left towards the last week of September, mind you not before we received more clothes, some worn, some altered, and some as they explained, just for the purpose of exchanging them for other goods. They packed a big parcel of food and gave us orders to watch out for bad people, etc. Pani Oma said, "You find all sorts of people nowadays, so watch out, don't do anything stupid again. We will not be there anymore to help you."

"Our" officer came to give us another letter from his office and told us to only show this one if we were really in trouble. We promised. He stroked my hair and gave my mother his hand to say good-bye and then he mumbled in German, "It was a pleasure to have met you both. Godspeed!" And that was the last time we ever saw him.

The morning we had to leave was cold already, so we wore whatever we could to stay warm. This also helped the old suitcase that we got from Pani Oma so that it wouldn't break apart!

The good-byes were quick. We all had tears in our eyes but made sure that our emotions were under control.

Mr. Anaszevich drove us with the horse and buggy to the train station and when the train arrived, he didn't stay long. He looked so sad when he gave me his last hug. My tears came down uncontrollably but we had to rush to get on the train because it was crowded and people pushed to get in. Minutes later we were on our way.

At least that's what we thought.

Free, but among prisoners

THE FIRST HOUR OR SO WAS FINE. MIND YOU, WE COULDN'T understand much of what these people were talking about because everybody spoke Russian or Polish. But we were free, not in prison anymore; we would be home soon and therefore, so what! My mother reminded me to be brave and said, "We will make it."

The train stopped quite often and more and more people, children, chickens, ducks, and even a goat came on board. My mother and I held onto each other and we didn't speak until somebody pushed more and more and my mother lost my hand. She called me and then said in German that I must come back to her. And suddenly everybody was staring at us and somebody said, "Germans," and pointed towards us. Instantly we became enemies and somebody must have called the police because at the next stop we were taken off of the train.

Oh God! We were scared. Anyway, one of the policemen patted us up and down to make sure that we weren't carrying any weapons and then we were pushed with a rifle into a little train station. In there two Russian soldiers were sitting very comfortably in their chairs, both smoking and obviously joking around.

They hardly paid any attention to us until the policeman we came in with brought us to their attention and informed them what had taken place on the train. He pointed to us and all we understood was that we were in danger. One of the soldiers got up and must have asked the Polish policeman if we had shown any papers because he turned to us and asked in broken German if we had a passport or other documents. My mother showed him the document she had received from Mrs. Anaszevich. They looked at the papers and discussed the matter between them and then the policeman turned to us and said, "Not good, you come with me." I looked at my mother and we both had tears in our eyes and while we were still standing there not really moving but now being pushed, my mother said, "Wait a minute. I have another document." And she gave them the letter from "our" officer. They looked at this document and after a long while one of them went to the telephone. We heard him talking and then he must have been put on hold. After a moment or so he spoke again, this time very formally and obediently. After he hung up, he came back and looked at us as if we had come from the moon. In his broken German he told us we would have to stay overnight until a train with German war prisoners arrived. He said, "Usually they don't stop here but tomorrow, because of you, the train will stop to pick you up." He continued, "This train is going to Germany, to Berlin, and will take you where you want to go." He spoke to the Polish policeman and told us to go with him. We wondered where we were being taken and my mother, now more hopeful that we would continue our trip soon, asked him where we would be staying while we waited for this train. He looked bored and pretended he didn't understand what she was talking about. So he didn't explain but instead just said, "Go. Go with the policeman. Now!" Instead, my mother shook her head and asked him to return our papers to her. She said it in a very demanding tone and he kind of smiled at her, and for a moment or so, I thought he would not return the papers, but he did. He hesitated, but he did give her back all of the papers, which we realized were very important for us to have, especially the letter from Mikhail.

We were brought to the waiting room of the train station and were told not to move until we were called. There were a few other people, but all spoke Polish. My mother and I didn't speak at all; we didn't want to make the same mistake again.

We became hungry, but we didn't open our parcel packed with food, because maybe this too would have caused attention. We played it low this time; we had learned our lesson. And then I became very tired and soon fell asleep. When I woke up I didn't realize that we had waited almost twelve hours for this other train to come. My mother was completely exhausted holding me and watching the few belongings we had brought with us. She whispered that two trains had passed already but, until now, we had not been called and she was praying that they would send us on our way soon.

About an hour later we heard a train coming in again and minutes later we were called out.

We saw this big freight train standing there. Out of the roofs of the box cars came tin pipes and it looked like these pipes came from stoves. Stoves in a train? I found this funny until one of the guards from the station pushed open a big door and we were asked to enter. My mother argued that this was the wrong train, but we were pushed to get up, and so we had no other choice but to go on.

The smell was awful and sickening and the men who were in there were dirty, sick, and so undernourished that one could see all their bones. Their faces were skulls covered with skin and their eyes were big but surrounded with almost black circles. They looked so awful that it gave us the shivers. My mother said to me that cattle are transported much more humanely than these poor men.

Actually there was no space for us. The straw was filthy and full of human waste because all of them had diarrhea and there was vomit everywhere. They had pails but these were full and most of them could no longer make it to them anyway.

We were standing there not saying a word but my mother's eyes filled with tears. We figured that all of them were prisoners of war and were being sent home and when my mother asked them, they confirmed this. "Yes, we all come from Siberia and became sick while in camp. They sent us home because they were ordered to release some prisoners and since we were useless and couldn't work anymore they stuffed us like cattle in these box cars. Every so often they stop the train to get the dead out and to give us some water and what they call soup. However, the soup is more or less water too. You are lucky if you find three or four beans in it and you are even more lucky if you find a piece of potato. Every third day we receive one loaf of bread for five people. We had it bad in camp, but at least we could go out. Now we hardly see the sun or the moon anymore. Every two weeks or so they let us change the straw and the pails. We have been traveling like this for three months now."

But one man said, "Germany lost the war and we should be glad if we make it home at all."

They made a corner for us and we sat down. It was so awful that it took us a long time to get the smell out of our noses. (And we thought that we had it bad in jail and in the camp!) My mother told me not to touch anything because she thought they had typhoid fever. I tried not to touch anything but of course this was hard to do.

We settled down and were cold instantly. One of the soldiers said that they ran out of wood for the little pipe stove but as soon they stopped again, and hopefully this would be soon, he would try to get some and this would make a difference. However he said, "It will stink more." But jokingly he continued, "Many have died from being cold but nobody has died yet from the stench. We don't smell it at all anymore and you will get used to it too."

"Where is your home?" somebody asked. My mother answered Berlin. "Well, I think we are close to the German border. What was the name of the station where you came on board?" But my mother shook her head saying that she didn't know. "I didn't even look." And then she told them what happened to us and from where we came. They listened and one of them said, "You were lucky that they let you go with this train. It could have been worse for you and, if we are all lucky, we will get home at least some day, who knows when. By the way, your papers must be good, don't let them out of your hands."

By now I was very hungry. After all we hadn't eaten or had much to drink for two days. My mother asked them if they had some water for me but they answered that they would not recommend drinking it. "If you can wait until the afternoon, maybe they will give us fresh water and, if we are lucky, we will get some soup, more water." Most of them laughed at that remark.

After a while I asked my mother if maybe we could open the parcel we received from Mrs. Anaszevich. She looked at me and realized that I was desperate to have some food. And then she looked at all the men; I think there were twenty or so still sitting up and many more who just lay almost lifeless in the dirt. She whispered, still holding onto the parcel, "If I open it we have to share and I don't know what and how much is in it."

"Mutti," I said, "I am so hungry and why don't you want to share?"

She answered, "You are right." And then she asked if somebody could help her open the parcel.

The one soldier who talked to us before and who must have been the spokesman agreed to help. He came over to us and asked, "Who gave you the parcel?" It was quite big and was heavy. My mother told him where we got it and again he said, "You are so lucky. You must have met really kind people." And then he worked on the parcel. He made sure not to rip the cord and not to damage the carton.

We all were curious to see what Mrs. Anaszevich had packed for us and when he finally opened it, we were all speechless. There was bread, sausages, cheese, butter, sugar, preserves, and a chocolate bar with my name on it. It was amazing! My mother told them that she would share some of this parcel with them, but first she had to give some food to me. Of course they all agreed, but they now came very close to our corner and waited for their turn. And once I had some food, she started to share and after an hour or so everyone had received some of everything and we all had a feast. My mother warned them not to eat all of their share at once, but many did and they were sick as dogs a bit later.

My mother kept some for us and had to guard the little that was left very closely. The eyes of the soldiers were constantly on the magic parcel and it was hard for my mother to resist these sad eyes and not give all of it to them.

In the afternoon the train came to a stop and the doors were opened one by one. There were Russian soldiers all around the train and all of us had to step out and stand in a row in front of each wagon. When they saw my mother and me, they told us to step away from the group and an officer came directly to us to asking what we were doing among these prisoners. My mother gave him our precious letter to read and after a while we were told to step back to the rest of the group. However, he wanted to keep the letter. My mother told him that she would not leave until he returned the document. She continued in saying to him to call the person who had signed the letter. He looked at her as if he wanted to hit her but read the letter again and then with a big grin on his face he said in broken German, "You sleep with him?" He thought he made a big joke because he suddenly laughed so loud that everybody looked at us. "You so lucky I am in a good mood today." And then he returned the letter and let us go back to the group and later back onto the train.

After about ten days or so we arrived in Berlin. By now we were both sick too, but still, we made it home. We had lice and fleas and were sprayed again as soon we came off the train. The powder was so itchy and after a while I had a rash again. My body was full of little blisters and I was crying. My mother told me to stop and pointed to the sign that said Berlin.

I think the station where the train stopped was called Schlesischer Bahnhof but I am not sure anymore. The most important thing for us was that we were home and that we had made it. I stopped crying but I was very sick and in pain and I think so was my mother. The bandage that she always wore to stop the swelling of her leg started to show that the wound on her ankle had opened up again. Of course, I felt bad, and was afraid that she would tell me again that it was my fault because it started after I was born. And the agony we both had to go through until we arrived here didn't help. I felt it was my fault.

We made it, but to what?

WE HAD TO GO THROUGH SEVERAL CONTROL STATIONS BUT I guess our papers were good. They let us go out on the street. The station had been bombed and there was no clock, so we had no clue what time it was.

We must have arrived early in the morning because not many people were on the street yet. What street? Everything was in ruins; there was almost nothing left of what we would have remembered. My mother took me by my hand and tried to find out where we were. She asked a woman who was passing how we could get to the district and street where we used to live. The woman was friendly enough and told us that we were very far away from the address my mother gave her. She said there were not many transportation possibilities left and the best thing was to walk until we found a policeman who could help us. She walked on wishing us good luck.

We stood there somewhat helpless and cold. It was the 26th of October, 1945. We realized that Germany was definitely defeated and learned later that Hitler capitulated on April 30th, 1945, and not, as we were told by some Russian soldiers in Poland, in January.

However, they were correct that there was more or less

a bloodbath before Hitler finally gave up and committed suicide in his command bunker in Berlin. He was found by Russian troops with his mistress Eva Braun, both shot and set on fire outside the bunker.

After April 30th, some Germans still continued to resist, especially the very young who were hardly more than children and had been enlisted at the very end. But eventually everyone surrendered on May 2nd, 1945, and with that the war was finally over. Officially, Germany surrendered unconditionally on May 7th, 1945, in Reims, and the documents were signed during the night of May 8th to May 9th in Soviet headquarters–Berlin.

It is written that the war in Europe lasted five years, eight months, and six days. Germany lost 2.85 million soldiers and half a million civilians. And, of course, there were uncounted misplaced people as well.

The Allies had suffered equally. It was the second world war and it was hoped that it would be the last.

On June 5th Germany was divided into four zones, the three western to the Allied forces: the American, British, and the French; and the East to the Soviets. However, at first, Berlin was under total control by the Soviets, until July, when it was divided into four sectors. The British and Americans took command of their sectors at once. The French followed in August.

Berlin had approximately 1.5 million people fewer than when the war began. But there were still about 2.8 million people living in the remaining ruins. The centre of the city was more or less all rubble, yet the outskirts of Berlin were still somewhat recognizable. In principle, however, Berlin had been bombed to the ground and most people were without homes, water, and heat. The word food was almost foreign and for us, it was all overwhelming.

My mother told me that we had to walk and find somebody who could at least tell us in which direction we must go. So we walked. Our luggage and especially the parcel were light now but so were our shoes. My feet were freezing and the sores I had on them had started to hurt again. The wounds were closed but the scars still looked red and as soon my feet became cold the pain would come back. I shivered but my mother told me to stop complaining. She said, "We have made it this far and now we will make it home. Your feet will be looked after as soon we can but right now I can't help you. I am in pain too but we have to go on. Be glad we are back home."

And so we walked until I couldn't go on anymore and started crying. I couldn't help it; not only was I tired and hungry but my feet were in really bad shape. My mother didn't know what to do with me anymore. Naturally she was frustrated and so we just sat down right in the middle of the sidewalk, whatever was left of it.

Many people passed us without looking at us. Everybody looked the same, dirty, undernourished, and hopeless. We saw mostly women. The few men we noticed were either old or invalids. But all looked sick, cold, and lost.

As we sat there, an old man came towards us and asked my mother why I was crying and if he could help. My mother got up and told him that his concern was really appreciated and then asked if he could tell us how we could get to our home since we had just arrived from Poland and were totally lost. He was not quite sure himself, but while they were talking, a policeman came and stepped into the conversation. Mother explained our situation again to him and he suggested that we take the streetcar, which came by once in a while and it would at least bring us a bit closer to where we needed to go. He asked my mother if she had money for the fare and after she told him that we had nothing, he gave it to us. He said, "The money is worthless, but it is still good for some things. I hope you and your little daughter will make it home soon. And by the way, you are still in the Russian sector, but the street you mentioned is located in the American sector." He smiled, "Later you will realize that you will be in the better sector. The Americans are nicer to us losers. Make sure you arrive there before it gets dark and before the curfew is in effect. The Russian militia is very strict and you would have a lot of explaining to do. The Americans are more understanding, but still, make sure you make it in time."

Of course we didn't know what he was talking about. Curfew and what was a sector? Are there soldiers in Berlin other than Russians? My mother was puzzled, but we had no time to ask questions. We had to try to get home.

We walked on and finally saw a streetcar stop. We waited in line with many people and while we were waiting, more and more people joined us. My mother started talking to one woman and explained to her again where we had come from and where we wanted to go. She was kind and tried to help and involved others. She explained that we were somewhat lost and confused. Everybody had some bits of advice until one woman stepped forward and told us to try to get a taxi.

My mother asked, "Are there still taxis around? And where would we get one, we have no money."

The woman answered, "I will get us one and because

I have to go almost the same way we could share the fare. Once you are home you can get the money and you can pay me your share. I will give you my address and I am sure you will pay me back."

But my mother didn't trust her and argued that we didn't even know if the apartment building was still there. The woman realized that my mother didn't trust her and just said, "Suit yourself" and left.

I think my mother offended her. In the meantime the streetcar arrived. But it was so crowded with people, some hanging almost outside, that only a few were able to get on. So we were still standing there and were even more discouraged.

The woman who had asked us to share a taxi was almost out of sight. She was already walking on the other side of the street and was ready to turn a corner when suddenly my mother called after her and we ran to catch up with her.

My mother cried out to her to stop and wait for us and so she did. When we reached her, my mother asked her if the offer still stood and if we could go with her. She said, "Of course, but I had the feeling you didn't trust me. Did you change your mind?" She didn't wait for an answer and continued, "So, all right, we will find a taxi."

My feet got worse. I could hardly walk anymore but walk we had to do. For at least twenty minutes or so and then we saw a car. The driver, an old man with dirty, ripped-up clothes, was smoking a funny cigarette. It was rolled in newspaper and it smelled awful. It reminded me of our camp in Poland where the Russians smoked almost the same kind.

He was a friendly, older man and smiled when he saw

us. And obviously he knew the woman we came with. He asked her, "The usual way?"

"No, not this time. If you could, would you bring us first to Harzer Strasse, Neukoelln?"

He looked at us and asked her who we were and where she found us. She explained and since it was out of his way she wanted to know how much extra it would cost to bring us to our apartment. She told him that she wanted to help us. They went back and forth about the price and we knew it was a lot. But it wasn't money they bartered about, yet the woman finally agreed and we got in.

He started the car and the motor wouldn't turn. He got out, swore, and opened the hood and after working for a while on the motor he started the car again, but still it wouldn't turn over. He swore again, and said "shit" a lot and tried again. And after a few more times and a lot of "shit", it turned over and we heard the sweet sound of the motor. For me it was exciting again because I remembered my first car ride on our way to Poland.

But what we saw during the ride was awful. The city was in ruins and there was no hope it would ever recover. The driver asked us about our trip and again my mother told him from where we had come. And after a long pause he said, "You are so lucky that you made it. I lost my family and my grandchildren just a few months ago. Our apartment building was bombed to the ground. I have nothing left but this old car, now my home. Yes, you are lucky." He continued, "Many here have died or the ones who went to the East were murdered. Yes, be thankful to be here and alive." My mother didn't answer but knew he was right.

After we drove for quite a while he started talking to

the woman who helped us to find this taxi. We couldn't understand what they were talking about, but they were laughing and sounded happy.

She was actually well dressed compared to all the other people we saw and we wondered who she was and where she came from.

My mother noticed a big sign that read "You are now entering the American Sector" and a bit later we saw soldiers in a completely different uniform. Compared to the Russians they looked very well dressed and clean. They made us stop and our driver talked to them and said something we couldn't understand and the woman smiled and they smiled back and waved us through. My mother asked what this was all about and they explained that we were now in the American-controlled part of Berlin, which was good and we should be glad to live here rather than in the Russian sector. We still didn't understand what that meant.

We drove on and not too long after, we saw the street sign Harzer Strasse and my mother screamed, "This is our street. We live here, Harzer Strasse 92." And again, "We live here! We made it. We're home!"

The front building was still standing almost without damage, only the windows had cardboard or wood rather than glass and the façade was covered with gun holes or something. But the building itself was standing.

How would the back building be? We didn't care at this moment, we were just so happy to be home. The woman got out of the car and opened the door for us. My mother wanted to ask her to wait here. She wanted to see if she could get money from my father. She was for some reason sure he would be home, waiting for us. But the woman just said, "I am glad you made it and maybe we will meet again one day and then you can pay me back." My mother couldn't say a word and suddenly she just embraced her and had tears in her eyes. And when she found her speech again she said, "You are a good person. Thank you! Thank you so much."

The woman's face turned red. She was embarrassed but said to my mother, "I am glad I could help." Mother continued in asking her for her name and address, but again was told not to worry. "Be happy that you made it, I wish you luck. As I said, maybe one day we will meet again."

And by the time I got out of the car and we looked around, they were gone. We never did see her again.

We went through the big front door into the inner dark hall, carried on to the small door, and came into the courtyard. It was late afternoon by now and a grey day. The back building was still standing too, but only up to the second floor, our floor. The third and fourth floor and the roof were bombed and missing. All the windows were damaged, some still open and some covered up with cardboard. The courtyard was full of deep craterlike holes.

But we hardly noticed anything. We just held our breath and ran up to the apartment. My mother knocked a few times because the bell was not working. No answer. She knocked again, this time much louder and just when she was ready to give up, my stepfather opened the door. They looked at each other and then he said, "Rosi, what are you doing here? I didn't hear from you and I thought you were both dead." His voice was cool. There was no sign that he was glad to see us.

After a moment he asked us to come in and looked

at me and said, "You have grown." But he didn't hug me. My mother wanted to go straight to the living room but my father held her back saying, "Wait a minute, I have to clean up a bit. I wasn't expecting you."

My mother just smiled and opened the door. She went in and came right out again, screaming at him, "You are sleeping with another woman. She is lying in our bed!" She clawed him right across his face and screamed, "You pig you! You had her here all the time while we were gone. Didn't you?" He tried to calm her down and wanted to explain but she wouldn't listen.

I started to cry but nobody paid any attention to me. They were absorbed with themselves, fighting and screaming, and then my mother went back into the room and wanted to attack the woman she saw in their bed, but Papa stopped her by holding her back. He wanted to calm her down but she hit him again. We went to the kitchen and he said very calmly, "Our marriage is over, Rosi, there was never love between us and you must look for a different place to live. For tonight you can stay here in the kitchen with Steffie but that is all I can offer you. If you want to, you can leave Steffie with me. As you know, she was always welcome here. I love her like I would love my own child."

And mother continued the sentence by saying, "Which you couldn't make, you drunkard! You were not able to make a baby so you thought you could pretend you have one by giving Steffie your name." She didn't cry but looked wild and so she just took me by my hand and we left. We almost flew down the stairs and out of the building into the front hall. There, my mother started to cry. I saw the pain in her face and I felt so sorry for us and suddenly I said, "We should go and find Mutti."

My mother looked at me and said, "You mean Meta?" And I answered, "Yes."

My foster mother is alive

WE WALKED DOWN THE STREET AND WONDERED HOW WE would make it to "my Mutti", when we saw a streetcar coming. The streetcar would bring us half way to Woernitzweg, where we would hopefully find her.

We ran to the stop and made it. We hopped on and when we found a seat I whispered to my mother, "Do we have money to pay the fare?"

And my mother whispered back, "Yes, remember we still have the money the policeman gave us. We wondered why the streetcar was almost empty and when the conductor came by to collect the fare, my mother asked him if we were in the right streetcar. He confirmed that we were and so for about fifteen minutes we relaxed. My mother gave me the almost empty parcel and she held onto the suitcase, which was in bad shape by now. As we drove on we saw that the area we had known for so many years was more or less unrecognizable. The ruins here were so overwhelming. There was really nothing that was left undamaged but people seemed to accept it, or had to, in order to live on. We wondered that the streetcar was still running and the conductor told us that some worked fine but most were completely destroyed and they only ran if the electricity was on. So we were lucky, he said.

We made it to Karl Marx Strasse and got off. We still had to walk for about twenty-five minutes or so. My toes hurt so much that I was so tempted to start crying. However, I didn't say a word. I was eager to get to "my Mutti", who, I was so sure, would be there for us. I just hoped that she would remember us.

When my mother pressed the outside bell, I was praying that my Mutti would respond with the buzzer to let us in. But we didn't know that that area had no electricity and Mutti didn't hear us, and we were not able to enter the apartment building unless somebody would come with a key or would open the door from the inside. We had no other choice than to wait. And wait we did. It became very cold and it was dark and we were so tired that we sat down on the outdoor step for some time when, unexpectedly, we saw the street lights come on and the street come to life. We tried the doorbell again and as an answer we heard the little noise, the buzzer, and my mother pushed the door open.

We entered and saw my foster mother standing there and I wanted run up to her and hug her, but she looked so different from how I remembered her. She was still tall, but her hair was grey and she looked skinny and frail. I hesitated to run up because I guessed she didn't recognize us at first either, or maybe she was surprised to see us. I looked at her and then I saw a big smile come over her face and she called out, "Steffchen, my Steffchen, is it you?" And then I ran into her arms and we didn't let go of each other until my mother made a little noise as if to say, "I am here too." Of course my foster mother reached out to her as well and mumbled, "This is a dream. Stef-fchen, you are alive and Rosi, you too, it is not a dream!" And she asked us to come in. And so we walked into the so familiar little hall.

My mother told her briefly what happened to us a couple of hours earlier, and then she asked her if we could stay for a few days to sort things out and find a resolution as to how we would be able to carry on. As my mother explained to my foster mother, Meta, "At this point I am at the end of my rope. I didn't expect Richard to have another woman living there. I hope you can help us out."

Of course, my Mutti said, "Stay as long as necessary." She still had her loving heart and open door for every-body who was in need of her help, regardless of whether she had been hurt by this person or not. She was still the amazing human being I remembered and loved so much.

She asked us to step into the living room and when we entered we were surprised by what we saw. The furniture had all been replaced by four rows of theatre seats. They were placed around a pipe stove with the pipe directed right through the room towards one of the two windows. This window was covered with some strange material, fire resistant she explained, and obviously it did the trick. The room was warm and about eight neighbours were sitting around the stove, some reading, some preparing a meal peeling half-frozen potatoes and so on. Many recognized me and said, "You must be Steffie. God, have you grown! You look like a little lady now." And I was happy and pleased to hear their compliments.

My mother asked my foster mother where all her furni-ture had gone and my foster mother smiled and answered, "I will burn most of it. The winter is coming soon so I made firewood out of it. It is all stored in the basement where, by the way, we all still sleep. We have the beds down there in the rooms that used to be our bunker. It is really not too bad and warmer than up here where all the windows are missing or covered with cardboard. I found the glass you see in this one window here in the ruins. It was a miracle. It was not broken and fitted nicely."

The two of us were amazed and couldn't close our mouths. And then my mother came back to reality and said, "So you made firewood out of most of your furniture just to keep warm and help your neighbours?"

"Yes, Rosi, I did, and so did many others. If we want to survive we have to do these things. I am sure you had to do things too to survive. But we will talk about it later. I am sure you two went through hell. Both of you look like it."

As we made ourselves a bit comfortable, the neighbours left one by one, as Mutti explained, to make use of the electricity. She told us that the lights would stay on for only about two hours and it changed every week. Time is precious when we have electricity. When it comes on during the night we set the alarm clock and do what we have to do during the night. We must make the most of it whenever we have electricity. It is almost like a lifeline. We breathe normally when we have electricity and save the breath when we have to sit in the dark or by candlelight. Since we don't have many candles or fluid for the petroleum lamps we sit most of the time in the dark."

I noticed while the neighbours were still there that they called my Mutti "Muttchen" rather than Frau Pech or Meta. I liked that because it would be better for me if I would call her Muttchen too. I was sure my mother would like it and wouldn't get angry when I called both Mutti. I asked Muttchen if she would mind and she didn't. I told her I would only do it if both Muttis were together and they both smiled. But, of course, from then on I called her Muttchen or sometimes Momutch. She really loved it when I called her Momutch.

I suddenly realized that my foster father was missing. Muttchen noticed that I seemed fidgety and asked me if I wanted something and I shook my head. But then I asked her where Papa was. She became very sad and answered that he was not with us anymore, he was with the angels now.

She didn't realize that I knew more about dying than I should have at my age. So she was surprised when I looked straight into her eyes and said, "Was he shot by Russians? They do that, you know. We saw them doing it."

But she explained that he died in July 1943 in the boiler room. "It was an accident. He was overcome by fumes while looking after the central heating and the hot water supply. It was so sad. Before he left he told me that there was some gas leaking out of the boiler but he fixed it. Well, it probably was not fixed properly. They said he was poisoned by carbon monoxide. He probably noticed something and wanted to get out but it was too late. He was not able to open the door anymore. We found him right behind the big heavy iron door where he had collapsed. It was a terrible accident."

I started to cry but she told me not to be sad because, she continued, "As I told you, he is with the angels in heaven now and probably is as glad as I am to have you back."

I wanted to talk about him a bit more but my mother stopped me by saying, "You have to go to bed soon. It has been such a long day."

Muttchen agreed and said, "Yes, we all have to go to bed because even though the electricity is still on, we have to conserve, and since all the things we had to do are done, we will go to bed because we have to save wood too. Come, I will boil some water so you can wash up a bit and after that we will go down. I promise you, you will sleep like my little baby again."

When I undressed, she saw my feet and kind of shrugged. She made me soak my feet for a while, put some ointment on and bandaged them. It hurt awfully at first but a bit later it felt good. She did the same with my mother. She gave her fresh bandages and also some of the ointment and said, "You both have to see a doctor. Steffchen is so skinny that she looks like a leaf in the wind and you have skin like a woman who is eighty." We all laughed but I think it was not a laughing matter.

My foster mother got some clean sheets from somewhere and the three of us went down into what used to be the bunker. The bunker was divided in sections and in each section were at least two to four bunk beds, a few shelves, a table, and some chairs. Everything was more or less just put together but it was better than what we had had in Poland in jail and in camp.

We had a section with two bunk beds and my mother wanted to put me on the top of her bed, but I wanted to sleep on top of my Muttchen's bunk. My mother was not pleased, but my foster mother said, "Let her be for tonight. Tomorrow she will sleep above your bed." But I never did.

At last we felt safe again

I woke up and for a moment I didn't know where I was. I started to scream but my mother was up already and whispered that we were all right. She reminded me that we were safe and with my foster mother. I fell back into my blanket and asked if she was still sleeping.

"No," my mother answered, "she got up a long time ago. She told me she had to go "shopping". It was dark where we were but there was a lamp lit in the other section, which gave us a little light and gave me some comfort. I wanted to go upstairs so my mother lit another little lamp filled with petroleum. She told me that my foster mother left it for us. We went to the other section to blow out the petroleum lamp there and then my mother took me by my hand and we went upstairs to the apartment to get dressed.

The pipe stove was doing its job already and a few neighbours sat around it to warm their fingers. They had all slept downstairs in the bunker, but I hadn't heard or seen them. I guess everybody had their little privacy down there.

The winter had started already. It was cold outside and because there were hardly any windows, it was damp and cold inside as well.

We said good morning and went to the bathroom to wash up. We had no toothbrush and no comb but at least we had some cold water. When we came back to the room we noticed how pale and undernourished everyone looked, but nobody complained. As a matter of fact they kind of looked happy and had a smile for us. They asked a lot of questions, but Mutti didn't say much. She wanted to tell Muttchen the details first.

A bit later Muttchen returned and we learned what shopping really meant in Germany in the year 1945.

Muttchen explained that she had gone to the black market to get some sugar and bread for us. She looked worried. She told us that everything was so expensive and people took everything they had to the black market to exchange it for food. "The stamps we get from the government are too much to die on and not enough to live on. I just exchanged my earrings for two pounds of sugar and two dark rye breads. Tomorrow we get new ration stamps and then I must see how we will manage." And she continued, looking at my mother, "You must go to city hall today to fill out all the documents necessary to get ration stamps for the two of you. The rations for Steffie would be a bit better than the base card for adults, which is only six hundred calories per day. A child gets a thousand per day. She also will get milk rations, which she sure needs."

My mother promised to go out a bit later. She also wanted to find out how to get a divorce. But Muttchen didn't think this was important and said, "Don't you think this still has some time, Rosi? Get all the papers you need to stay and to get the ration cards first, and then you can go after your divorce."

"Also, you must try to get the apartment. But this will

all take some time. Just get your papers together. You need the ration cards in order to survive. Do you still have your old passport? You will need it."

I saw that my mother became upset. At first she didn't say a word but then she answered, "No, Meta, they took my passport a long time ago. I only have the papers they gave us to make it possible to return from Poland. I don't even know what the papers say because they are written in Polish, but wherever I have shown them they worked to let us come home."

Muttchen told her to try to get a new passport with these papers. "But don't let them out of your hands," she warned. My mother knew that from experience.

We had breakfast. Muttchen sliced two very slim slices of dark rye bread for each of us, toasted them on top of the pipe stove a bit and sprinkled some sugar on top. She then spread some paper out, turned the slices upside down and shook the sugar off again. She explained, "This will save some sugar but will still give you the taste of a bit of sweetness. It is better than eating it without anything, right?"

She also made tea, peppermint tea for me with half a teaspoon of sugar, for my mother and herself just plain. She told us that she got the tea from her little field close to where I was born. My mother asked her if the cottage was still standing and Muttchen nodded, "Yes it is, but we just use it as a shack. The most important thing is that we can plant vegetables and potatoes there. I also have some fruit trees. She smiled and said, "It all helps. I was so very lucky that the preserves I had stored in our basement were not found by the Russians. So we have quite enough vegetables and fruit for the winter."

My mother and Muttchen talked for a long time after

breakfast. Mutti told her what we had had to go through to get home again and in detail how helpful our officer and the Anaszeviches had been. And then she said to Muttchen that she was ashamed for what she had done to her and that she was truly sorry and very thankful that we could stay here for a while. Muttchen just answered, "I am happy to be able to help."

My mother showed her what was left in the parcel and what we had in the suitcase we got from the Anaszeviches. There were some things that could be exchanged for food but mostly there were clothes we needed to get through the winter. The food from the parcel was welcome and would help a bit to ease the need for food without having the ration cards.

It took over three months for us to get our full ration cards. First we received provisional ones that were almost half of what we would have received if our status had been accepted, but, as with all governments, they took their time. My mother said that it was because we didn't return to my stepfather, to our original address. But during these weeks, where we had absolutely nothing, my Muttchen carried us through by exchanging her last possessions for food.

Back to school

ABOUT TWO WEEKS AFTER OUR ARRIVAL MY MOTHER AND Muttchen mentioned that I had to go back to school. Instantly I said, "I don't want to go." I explained, "They will all laugh at me as they did in Poland."

My foster mother looked at my mother and Mutti told her what had happened to me and that Mr. Anaszevich had actually rescued me from the cruelty of those children by asking the principal to excuse me from the school altogether.

So Muttchen said to me, "Steffchen, you have to go to school. Nobody will give you a hard time. All of the children here are in the same situation. You will see. You must go; you want to learn how to read and write properly, don't you?" I guess I agreed to go and the next day my mother and I went to the school I had actually attended before we were evacuated. It was just so much closer.

The school had been bombed too, but nonetheless was still in service. Most of the windows were covered with boards or something like plastic. They had fixed everything provisionally so that the children could have some instruction. We saw the same pipes sticking out of the windows as we had at Muttchen's place. My mother said,

"I wouldn't be surprised if they have stove pipes in the classrooms as well." And they did.

It was a long interview because the principal didn't know in what grade she should put me. There were no records left anymore because of the bombing and parts of the building were in complete ruins. I was now nine years old and had missed about two months of Grade Two and had no school at all in Grade Three. But my mother didn't agree with the principal that I should start with Grade Three again. She explained our situation and asked if the children here, during the capitulation, were able to attend school. And if not, were they all set back a year to complete their grades.

The principal answered, "No, of course not, but we opened the schools again in May and offered a catch-up curriculum."

So my mother said, "Could you not do that with Steffie as well? I am sure she, too, could catch up. She is very intelligent and I think you should give her a chance."

The principal, an older woman, her hair in a bun, so skinny that you could have knocked her over with a feather, gave me a strict look and I felt shivers. All I wanted was to go home, I felt so unwelcome. And I was not surprised that she shook her head and said, "I don't know, you don't even have the proper papers yet."

But my mother didn't give up and pointed out to her that I was born in Berlin and that I went to this very same school just before we were evacuated. She continued in saying, "We will get the proper papers soon. We must, we don't have ration cards yet and live with her previous foster mother."

The principal looked up and said, "Foster mother?"

"Yes," my mother answered. "She was in foster care until she was almost four years old. Why?"

The principal looked at my mother skeptically.

My mother continued, somewhat irritated, "Because I was not able to look after her properly."

More to herself than to us the principal said, "Too bad, we don't have the history anymore, but anyway, I think she needs to get into school as soon as possible. Let's try. I have a young teacher who just finished teachers' college. Nowadays they only need three months to call themselves teachers. But we are so short staffed since we lost almost all of our male teachers during the war. She just started here last month and maybe she wouldn't mind taking on more work and could tutor Steffie for a few weeks. Yes, let's try," she said again. Then she shook hands with my mother and with me and out we went.

The next day my mother walked me over to the school. Of course I was afraid to say the least, but I didn't say a peep because I didn't want to upset my Muttchen or my mother.

My mother brought me directly to the principal, told me to be brave, and left. The principal took me by the hand and marched me to a classroom. As soon as we entered, all of the children got up and stood at attention. The teacher, Fräulein Schmidt, came toward us and smiled, saying, "You must be Steffie."

I curtsied and said nothing, while the principal released my hand. She didn't even look at me anymore but told Fräulein Schmidt, "You take it from here, I am sure she needs a lot of tutoring." And with that, the woman who made me shiver left.

I liked Fräulein Schmidt instantly and was very willing

to do what she suggested or told me to do. I had a hard time adjusting at first, but I made it and by spring of 1946 I did fit in. One day I came home with a letter to tell my mother that I could accelerate to Grade Four. Both my Muttchen and my mother clapped their hands and I was on top of the world.

As we approached Christmas 1945 it was bitter cold outside and Muttchen did what she could to keep the room warm. We still slept in our basement room and for my mother there was no end in sight as far as moving on. She started to get depressed and complained that she didn't know how to carry on. Muttchen told her to look around for work. "Rosi, that way you would get your ration cards and your proper papers quicker and then you could also file for divorce. You are a Red Cross nurse and nurses are needed. Go to the hospitals and ask if there are some openings."

But I guess my mother was not ready yet to look for a job. And to postpone that, she started to complain about her leg again. However, she couldn't see a doctor because our papers still hadn't come through.

In the meantime my foster mother had a hard time making ends meet and exchanged whatever she had for food to feed two people without ration cards. I still don't know how she did it.

I started to grow. My shoes became too small and the few things I had, like the dresses Oma Anaszevich had made for me and the pair of pants and the underwear I still had, all became too small. Some clothes were so worn that they became, as Muttchen said, "holy", meaning they were so full of holes they couldn't be mended any-more. Another thing was that some of our clothes were still painted with the swastika. My mother had tried to get rid of it by scratching the paint off with a small knife, but you could still see it and it was so upsetting to walk like that in public.

In time Muttchen found a dressmaker who turned the coats, where the turpentine was applied, inside-out, which made them almost new looking and we could walk unnoticed in the streets again. The dresses were fixed the same way except I grew out of them faster than they were ready to be worn again.

Muttchen also went to the black market and exchanged some of the dresses I brought with me from Poland for bigger sizes. Most of the time I didn't like what she brought back but I had to wear them. So I cried when I had to put on clothes that simply did not fit and looked not only awful but were big and baggy. But Muttchen said, "Stop crying, that was the best I could get." And so it went.

The shoes she got were half leather, half wood. They were not bad because the wooden soles kept my feet somewhat warm. The upper part was leather and the nice thing about it was that we could cut the toe out, should I need bigger shoes for the summer.

My mother hardly cared, she left everything to Muttchen. Somehow she had changed again. She criticized more than she approved and never said thank you to Muttchen for all the things she did for us.

Muttchen went often to the black market to buy food. I wanted to go with her but she said it was dangerous and I should stay away from all of that.

Sometimes she wouldn't get home on time because she got caught by the police. They would take everything away from her and she would come home empty-handed.

When this happened, she was so discouraged tears ran down her cheeks. And of course she and my mother stayed hungry and she would just put something together for me. "The child must eat, we will have to do without until tomorrow," she would say.

She never gave up.

Our first Christmas after the war in 1945

JUST A FEW DAYS BEFORE CHRISTMAS MY MUTTCHEN MENtioned that we needed a Christmas tree. My mother couldn't believe what she was hearing. "A Christmas tree is a luxury," she replied.

But Muttchen said, "We have to have one, not for us, but for Steffchen. I will get a tree no matter how." And like so often, shortly after that she left to go "shopping".

Normally she would return the same day, but this time she didn't return. We became worried when it started to get dark. Our worries grew by the minute and we were so afraid for her. She was gone too long. My mother managed to blame me. She said, "You know, she went because she wanted you to have a Christmas tree. It sure was not important, but no, she had to go, and maybe risked her life for you."

It was the first time that my mother blamed me for something again over which I had no control. But I guess she was worried and frustrated and so I didn't feel guilty.

When finally, after a day and a half, the key in the door turned and Muttchen came in, we didn't say much but just thanked God that she had returned and took her in our arms.

She looked tired but her eyes were so happy when she showed us a pine tree, so little but so pretty, our first Christmas tree after the war.

She took the tree out of my sight right away and locked it in our little spare room because, as she said, "You will see it again on Christmas Eve." She then went out with a pail to come back a bit later with the pail filled with sand. I asked her what she wanted the sand for and she just answered, "You will see on Christmas Eve."

As was our German custom, I was not allowed to see the tree until Christmas Eve, and Muttchen made sure that I really didn't see it before that night. I later realized she needed the pail of sand because she didn't have a proper stand anymore, and so she stuck the tree into the pail filled with sand. On Christmas Eve my mother and Muttchen brought the tree into the living room and when everything was ready for Christmas, I was allowed to come from the kitchen to the room to see the tree again.

It was the most beautiful little tree I had ever seen. It had no ornaments but little cotton balls all over it, like snowflakes just fallen from the sky. There was only one used candle, which brightened the whole tree and made it shine gloriously, and under the tree were two presents for me, a sweater and a little doll.

She had exchanged her wedding ring for the doll and the sweater, and for the tree she had gone by train to a forest, far, far away from where we lived. I liked the sweater, but I fell in love with the doll since I hadn't had a doll since we were captured in Poland.

Later she read us the Christmas Story from Luke 2,

1:20 and then we had a little feast, I think even real coffee but I can't remember that for sure anymore. However, I do remember that some of the neighbours joined us to celebrate and that we gave thanks for the little things we had. And I felt that this was my best Christmas with the most beautiful Christmas tree I had ever seen.

Again, like always, my Muttchen had given of her last possessions to make others happy.

We became citizens of West Berlin, Germany

Right after the new year we received our proper papers and with that the so-important ration cards. We had a big feast and celebrated our official homecoming. Even the neighbours, who of course still came to warm themselves, had a slice of bread with the usual few crumbs of sugar on top and a cup of peppermint tea.

My mother's leg became bad again, but now at least she was able to see a doctor. He gave her some ointment, but the wound remained open and it only healed properly just before she died.

The doctor saw me too and warned her that I was undernourished. He recommended that my ration card be increased and gave my mother a request for the Government to do so. She had to fill out papers but a few days later I received the increase, which helped us all. Later my foster mother would jokingly say that I was now the main breadwinner in the household, and I was proud.

Muttchen, however, still had to go to the black market because both she and my mother had the lowest rations you could get. The reason for that was that my foster mother's job was not paying much and not considered hard work. She had only the four remaining houses to clean; all the others were bombed to the ground. And my mother still had no job at all. If you had a job cleaning up rubble you would be in the highest category, receiving enough points to satisfy a family of three. However, not many women were able to take on the hard work. It was a man's job, except that there were not many men left. Many women did try and some succeeded.

One day my mother left early in the morning. She was gone before I had to leave for school. I asked Muttchen what she was up to since she hadn't told me where she was going. My Muttchen told me that she had to go to court and hopefully she would get her divorce soon. I was sad because I had neither seen nor spoken to my stepfather since that afternoon when we returned from Poland. But I didn't say anything and went to school. She was still not back when I came home from school and I started to get worried. But Muttchen calmed me down and then I told her that I missed my Papa and started to tell her how good he had been to me. I think she then realized what I had gone through before we were evacuated. "My mother is much better now, but I am so afraid that she will change again." The signs were there but not as bad as before. Muttchen reassured me that she would watch her and would never allow her to be mean to me again. However she continued, "It is not good that you can't see your Papa again but you must understand that what he did was bad. He should have waited for you and your mother but instead he got involved with another woman. I think it is right that Rosi is getting divorced."

My mother came home late that afternoon. She

looked tired and even more worn out than usual and she told Muttchen that the first hearing was over but that she had another court session in two weeks. She also said that she hoped that he didn't bring up the fact that she had reported him to the police in 1942.

I didn't understand what was going on and why my mother was so afraid but I remembered that the police had come to our house and that Papa had had to go to the police station.

My foster mother looked at her and asked, "What did you just say? You did what?"

Mutti started to tell her what she had done and said, "I did it because I thought if they would send him to war he would stop drinking. I know now that this was wrong but I didn't know any other way to stop his drinking and having affairs with other women. You know," she continued, "I didn't have a happy marriage. He started drinking after the first year or so we were married. I just stayed with him because he was so good to Steffie. He really was. And I think Steffie loved him too, I didn't want to take that away from her."

Again my Muttchen looked at her and asked her, looking her straight in the eyes, "Then why did you take her away from us? We loved her and she loved us, and you didn't give a hoot about it."

I realized that Muttchen had become angry and I started to get scared that they would start to fight and we would have to leave. But my mother didn't say anything back to her. Instead she started to cry so that I almost felt sorry for her.

My foster mother ignored the tears and continued by saying, "Do you really know what you were trying to do?

If he brings all of that up now, you will go straight to jail. Rosi, you tried to have him killed and now all he has to do is tell the authorities what you tried to do to him. Does he know the details?"

My mother answered quietly, "I don't know, I just hope he doesn't."

I didn't understand much of what was going on and what my mother had done but I suddenly remembered all the things my mother had done to me and then I was scared. I didn't want to have this ever happen to me, never again.

I went close to my Muttchen and she hugged me and gave me the warmth I had started to miss again.

My mother stood up to go out of the room but returned and said, "I can't speculate about this now but I hope it stays civil. All I want is a divorce and the apartment. Since Steffie is not legally adopted, Richard probably doesn't have to pay for her. We will see. Maybe I should get a lawyer." She left to go to the kitchen.

Two days later a registered letter from my stepfather's lawyer arrived. My mother signed for it and opened it with shivering hands. Muttchen was just coming in from cleaning the apartment buildings. She looked pale and tired but when she saw my mother she asked right away, "Is something wrong?"

My mother read the letter first and then handed it over to my foster mother. And while my foster mother was reading it my mother smiled and whispered to me, "Steffie, everything will be good. We will get the apartment."

I was alarmed and said, "You mean we have to move?"

"Yes," she answered, "Isn't it good!"

I looked in shock at my mother and then at my foster

mother and whispered to myself, "I will stay here. I will not go back there. I hated it there! I will not go back!"

My foster mother looked up and smiled too, "So you will get no money from him but the apartment. Rosi, this is good! Will you say yes to the settlement?"

"Oh yes, I will agree and if all goes well I will be divorced in two weeks."

"Oh, by the way," my mother continued, "since I don't have a job yet, could Steffie stay with you for a while? At least until I am settled?" My Muttchen agreed at once and I was so very happy that I hugged them both.

My mother went to the second hearing and since she agreed to everything written in the offer, they were divorced that very same day and a month later my mother moved back to our old apartment.

My foster mother still worked from morning to night to keep our apartment warm and to put food on the table. And she continued to look after the few remaining apartment buildings. She cleaned and shoveled the snow from the sidewalk and listened to everyone's complaints. She was so well liked and helped to keep everything together. At times she looked very tired but she never complained.

There were still people in our living room to warm up there and as soon I came home from school I was helped with my homework and was entertained with games and songs by these neighbours.

We still had only two hours of electricity and as soon it came on we had the two hours for ourselves because the neighbours went to their apartments to do their chores like cooking, ironing, and such.

When the neighbours were gone, Muttchen too would cook and clean or do laundry. Alone, however, we always had fun times and she joked and made me laugh a lot. She also made sure that I got washed and cleaned up. The bath tub was always filled with cold water as a reserve since the running water was often interrupted. Sometimes there was no water at all for days. But she never gave up and always found ways to survive and encouraged other people to do the same.

The winter of 1945–1946 was a bitterly cold one. Many people froze to death. In order to carry on with school we had to bring some wood or coal to class. We wore cut-off gloves and all the clothes we could manage to put on.

I was not bad in school and Fräulein Schmidt was amazed how quickly I was able to catch up. However, she was worried about me because I often kept to myself and didn't pay any attention to the other kids. She questioned me about it and I told her I was afraid they would pick on me as they had in Poland. Of course, she sent a letter to my foster mother and asked her for an interview.

Since Muttchen really didn't know all the facts, she asked me what this was all about and after a while I started to talk and told her about my constant fears that other children would make fun of me. And then again I begged her that I didn't want to go back to my mother and that I was scared that I would have to go back soon.

Muttchen was shocked that I was still scared of children since really nobody had done any harm to me. And when she met with my teacher and the principal she mentioned that she almost thought that I needed help. But when my mother came to meet with them as well, she didn't agree with my foster mother and said, "Give her time, she will get over it." And maybe she was right, because eventually I overcame the fear, especially when I met a girl who soon became my girlfriend. Her name was Marleen and she lived close by. The fear that I would have to live with my mother, however, never left me.

My mother found a job

My mother, after she moved to our old apartment, didn't show up for a while. I think she was looking for a job and had no time to visit.

When she finally showed up she looked happy. She told us that she was somewhat settled now and that Richard had left most of the furniture and household items in the apartment. The only thing she was still working on was cleaning up the mess he had left behind. "I tell you," and she made a face, "you have no idea how dirty everything was. Disgusting! But at least I have the apartment. Also, I will start working at the hospital in Neukoelln. I applied last week and was accepted at once."

Muttchen asked her when she would start and my mother told her, "In a week. I have to work shifts and I will start with the afternoon shift."

And then my mother looked at me and I was afraid of what would come next. But I was wrong and relieved to hear what she asked Muttchen. "Could Steffie stay with you?"

My Muttchen looked at her and said, "Yes, but for good or only for a short while?"

"Well," my mother answered, not letting me out of her

sight, "I guess for a while. I have received a letter from Children's Aid regarding the child support I had requested. I will meet with them tomorrow and see how everything will be handled. Maybe I should request that they send the money straight to you rather than to me. After all, for the time being, I would be glad if Steffie could stay with you."

But Muttchen asked again, "What do you mean for a while? I don't want Steffchen to stay here only for a short time and then you move her again to another environment. She just recovered from what you both had to go through. Let her stay here until she really has recovered from all her problems. As you know, I am pleased to have her and later if she wants, she can go back to you. But I think we should leave it as it is for now and later she should be able to choose."

My mother agreed at once and with a little smile mumbled, "I don't even know yet if I will get custody or if Children's Aid will keep it since they are paying child support. I will let you know." She looked at me and gave me a kiss and thanked Muttchen for looking after me and then left.

I was so happy that I could stay with Muttchen, maybe forever? My fear that my mother would change her mind again came back. Oh God, I would not know what to do! I didn't say anything to Muttchen. I kept it inside and just hoped that I could stay with her forever.

We didn't actually see my mother for a while and Muttchen said, "She is busy, it is not easy to start a new job."

A month later Muttchen received the first cheque for me. It was a very small amount and she mentioned that nobody could feed and clothe a child from it. So when my mother finally came to see us, she told her how small the amount was that she received for me. My mother was not surprised and promised that once she got her pay she would give her some money to make it easier to take care of me. My mother also mentioned that she would receive an increase in her monthly ration card. Muttchen was glad since my ration card had been lowered again because I had gained some weight.

To steal was not a bad thing in 1946

ON MARCH 19TH, 1946 WE CELEBRATED MUTTCHEN'S birthday and I met her two brothers and their families. They knew me from when I had lived with my foster parents before so when they saw me they were so surprised at how much I had grown and made a big fuss over me. I, of course, didn't remember anybody and was very shy and embarrassed at first. But soon I came out of my shell. It became a big party and I had no clue where all the food and even coffee and "Schnaps" came from. However, I learned that most of Muttchen's relatives lived on the outskirts of Berlin where they had a little parcel of land and had some chickens and rabbits and even a pig or two. They, too, exchanged goods on the black market. So they brought things with them as Muttchen's birthday present. I tell you, it was a feast and we all felt so rich.

The party went on until early in the morning. For some of the time we were almost in the dark but since all of our neighbours were invited too, we had many candles and it was great. I lost my shyness and danced to the songs they were singing. Uncle Paul and Uncle Willhelm made music with a comb and a washboard, and a pail and some spoons as drums. They were mostly all sitting on the floor because we didn't have many chairs, but nobody minded. We were so very happy to be together and I think also happy just to be alive.

I must have fallen asleep because when I woke, Muttchen had already cleaned up most of the mess and was in the kitchen, busy with the dishes.

She smiled at me when I came in and asked if I was hungry. "Look, Steffchen, we have some leftovers." She laughed, "I can't believe it; we normally never have leftovers. What a party this was."

I was always hungry and I would have liked to eat again, but I pretended that I didn't want anything because I knew we would have another meal from the leftovers, maybe for supper or so.

While she did the dishes, I cleaned the living room a bit and Muttchen was pleased with me.

We carried on in our set routine for a while. The neighbours still came to warm themselves up since the winter of 1946 was one of the worst ones Berlin had ever experienced so far. But spring was in the air and soon the neighbours would move back into their apartments and maybe we could move upstairs. Muttchen had already made such plans and by April she moved two beds into our little spare room.

The black market thrived and young girls were proud when they found an American soldier as a boyfriend. The people, of course, looked down on them, but it was more envy than anything else.

The summer of 1946 was hot and I found out that the children in our neighbourhood were all boys. So I had to play like a boy and had to lose my girlish behaviour very quickly. We played mostly in ruins and to this day I don't know how my Muttchen ever got me cleaned up.

We still had a big sandbox in our courtyard. Of course it was meant for the little kids but we played there too. During lunch hours, when the little kids had to take their naps, we prepared cakes for our "bakery store" that we would sell to the little kids once they came back to play again. As payment we would take little stones. The parents were all for it since it kept us busy. However, the mothers didn't know how we prepared our merchandise. Since we had no water we all peed into the sand and then formed our little cakes and breads. The boys, of course, were surprised that I had to squat. They wanted to know why, but I didn't tell them. One day while we were preparing our "dough", a mother came by. After that our business went bankrupt.

When Muttchen learned about what we had been doing she was upset with me. However, she was smiling when she told other people about our adventure.

I started to help her to collect all sorts of things out of the rubble, the main thing being wood. I climbed way up into the ruins to saw down two-by-fours and such. It was a wonder that I never got hurt. Once I fell two stories down and had a lot of bruises but that was all.

Whenever I brought something home she told me how proud she was of me even though she knew at times that I stole things. We were fighting for survival, so everything was acceptable. As long we didn't hurt others we were in the game.

In the summer we often visited Muttchen's brother and family and we always came back with something to eat. While there, I discovered a field with cabbage and, of course, I went there to get us some heads of white and red cabbage. What I didn't know was that it was Russian property and watched by soldiers. Just when I had about three cabbages in my arms, I was pulled up by my hair and a gun was pointed at me. I knew I was in trouble and had to get out of it quickly. So I smiled and gave the cabbage to him and said, "This is for you. As he let go of my hair I ran as quickly as I could and put myself flat on the ground. I think if he had wanted to he could have found me but after about ten minutes I crawled to the end of the field and ran home to my Muttchen's family. When I told them what happened my foster aunt said, "You have to go back tomorrow morning between six and seven. That's when they change guards. Nobody said you shouldn't go there anymore." So I went again and came home with a whole sack of cabbages.

My Muttchen said, "You are my brave Steffchen," and gave me a big kiss.

One day I had the idea that we needed some meat on the table so I caught five sparrows using breadcrumbs and a sling. Muttchen made soup out of them.

Fall came fast and my shoes became too small. Muttchen cut the front of the shoes out so my toes had more room but soon my feet became cold and with that the pain from the old frostbite in my toes started up again. Muttchen went to the black market but came back saying that she could get a used pair for two loaves of bread. So we went to see my mother and asked her if she could help out with two bread stamps.

Muttchen knew that my mother often sold her stamps since she was getting her meals from the hospital for nothing. But my mother looked at us and told her that she would but she couldn't, because she had sold the stamps already and bought something for her apartment. She offered to sell us one loaf for sixty marks rather than for the going price of eighty marks. Muttchen almost lost it and gave her a deadly look but in the end she paid her the sixty marks and exchanged something else from her possessions for the balance.

I knew then that my mother had changed back again to the person she was before, as I had feared she would. I hated her and swore I would never go back to her.

Muttchen is sick

THE WINTER OF 1947 WAS VERY COLD AGAIN AND WE HAD more snow in Berlin than we had ever seen before. Muttchen was responsible for clearing the sidewalks in front of the houses she cleaned and so she was out almost every morning by four or five o'clock to shovel the snow. It was hard work but it was part of her job.

She also had the pipe stove going again, but we slept upstairs in our spare room now. She found more glass in the ruins and we had glass windows. The pipe stove's pipe was guided through an air shaft of the central heating system, which was still intact. The neighbours came again and so nothing much had changed, but Muttchen looked tired and worn out. She coughed constantly and I was worried.

One day she came home and told us that she had found an old coal storage place. The coal on the ground was gone but she said when you dug deep, you could still find coal, a lot of coal.

The next day she took our little hand-cart, a pick, and a shovel and went to dig out the remaining hidden coal deep in the ground.

She went every day for almost a month and was even able to exchange some coal for groceries and other goods.

Muttchen of course came home sweaty and lost more weight but she didn't listen when our neighbours warned her that she would get sick and should stop for a while.

Our next-door neighbour, Frau Lemke, talked to her almost every day, but Muttchen wouldn't listen to one word of it. And so one night she came home and fainted. We were lucky, the electricity was on, but I was all alone with her and just managed to pull her to bed, and after that I didn't know what to do except scream for help. Frau Lemke heard me and came at once. She ordered me to run to the doctor, which I did as fast as I could. Since the doctor lived around the corner and knew Muttchen, she took her bag and ran with me back to our apartment were Muttchen, by now conscious again, fought for breath. She looked so awful, white and frail, and for the first time completely helpless.

I was so scared, what could I do? And suddenly I remembered other people who looked like her just shortly before they died. Oh God, don't let her die, don't take her away from me. "Please," I prayed, "Please!"

The doctor felt her sweaty forehead and told us that she had a high fever and after listening to her chest she said it was pneumonia.

There were no antibiotics or any other medication available that would help. The only thing we could do was to try to keep her temperature down by washing her constantly with cool water and making her drink a lot.

The doctor gave us a potion to help Muttchen breathe more easily and then she left us. It was a time I never forgot and it took Muttchen three months to recover, but she was never the same after that. She did, however, learn to know the kindness of others.

For months she was not able to work and the government put her on welfare.

For Germans at that time that was shameful, especially when you were as proud as she was. Neighbours helped her by putting some money or a loaf of bread, etc., in front of our door. We never found out who the donors were and she never had to say thank you to their faces, because she was simply too embarrassed. Much later she wrote a letter and thanked everybody for their kindness. She was not used to being on the receiving end. She only knew how to give.

During the time of her sickness I grew up very quickly. Not only did I steal, but I learned how to organize and to get wood and even split it in pieces. I learned how to start a fire and keep it going. I cleaned her, cleaned her spit pot, and washed the clothes she wore. And I started performing badly in my schoolwork.

My mother hardly came by, saying that she was too busy. We found out later that she had met a man and had become pregnant and didn't want to tell my foster mother.

Not once did she ask how we were making out or if she could help. The only thing she would say is, "Steffie, I am proud of you, you are looking after your foster mother really well." And then she would repeat, "I am proud of you." As if she would know what our needs were.

Muttchen became better in late spring and we often went to her garden and planted and watered in the hope that this little garden would produce enough fruits and vegetables to help us through the next winter again.

I was always very embarrassed when she collected horse manure for the strawberries. I would stay back and pretend that I didn't know her. So one day I stayed behind again, and she turned and yelled, "But you like the strawberries and eat them without any hesitation, don't you?" The people around us all smiled and I was even more embarrassed and never stayed back again when she collected horse manure in her special "shit bag" for our garden.

She was so funny at times. One day we walked to the garden again and there was an older man in front of us. I am sure that he must have seen better times and must have been well off before the war. But now his once tailored, expensive suit looked run down, was ripped, and was much too big for him. His shoes had holes and he looked hungry and worn out like the rest of us.

After walking for a while in front of us, he turned around slightly and maybe thought we were further behind him than we were and we wouldn't hear but he let one go and it was a loud one, I tell you. I started to giggle and so did Muttchen. And then she called after him by saying, "Mr., Mr., I think you lost something." He turned around and looked at her and then said, "You stupid woman you. It is the bread they feed us, you should be glad you don't have to smell it."

Muttchen laughed so hard that she had to bend down and then she said, "That will teach him not to fart in front of ladies." Again, I was so embarrassed for her but when I think about it now I still find it so funny, especially because there was not much to laugh about in those days.

My mother gets married and it becomes the old story

My mother came by and she looked like she had gained weight. Even I noticed it. Muttchen looked at her and questioned her about it but my mother told her it was fluid, fluid we all accumulated because of the way we were eating and the lack of proper nourishment.

"Rosi, don't tell me this is fluid; you're pregnant, aren't you?"

My mother wanted to deny it but Muttchen just said, "Tell me the truth, Rosi, you are at least four months' pregnant, right?"

And after a moment my mother started to sob and said, "Yes, Meta, I am pregnant. However, the doctors agreed to an abortion since my legs are getting worse by the minute and it would be too risky to continue the pregnancy to full term." And she continued, saying, "And this is the reason why I didn't want to tell you about it."

"You look big, Rosi, how far are you really?"

My mother answered, "Beginning of the fifth month."

Muttchen looked at her again, "What? My God, you

must feel the baby move already, why did you wait this long?"

"Because it takes so long to get approval from the panel of doctors," my mother replied.

"Rosi, did you think this through? This is not an abortion, this is murder!" My foster mother was furious. I had never seen her like that.

But she calmed down again and said, "You must know what you are doing. I still think you should have thought about it before you slept with whoever it was. And I shouldn't talk; I had my dealings with abortion too. Believe me, that is something I will never forget."

I was not quite clear on what they were actually talking about. I remembered that in the Polish camp the women talked about abortion all the time, but what did it really mean? I didn't want to ask.

Muttchen continued and asked, "Who is the father?"

And my mother answered, "You don't know him yet, but we want to get married soon."

When I heard "married", my world fell apart. Would this mean that she wanted me back, that I would have to move and leave my Muttchen again? But they both didn't look at me; they were too involved in their conversation.

Muttchen shook her head. I think she was more angry than surprised.

"Is that why you didn't come to see us for the last three months, Rosi, because you have a man in your life again? And you are pregnant? I should have known better." And more to herself than to my mother, she mumbled further, "And now an abortion in the fifth month. Oh God, Rosi, will you ever grow up?"

And then Muttchen looked at me and asked my

mother, "And what about Steffchen? Are you leaving her with me?"

My mother looked at me and answered, "If I could, yes, she should stay with you, Meta."

"All right then, Rosi," Muttchen said. "You do what you have to do." And I guessed that the subject was closed.

"Now tell us about the new man in your life."

And so my mother told us. His name was Willi Grund and he was ten years older than she was. He, too, was divorced and had a daughter who lived with her mother. She continued, telling us that they met at work about six months earlier. He worked as a male nurse.

"He moved to my place last month and we want to get married as soon as possible. But next week I have to go in for the abortion. After that I will introduce him to you and to Steffie. He is nice, not as good looking as Richard was, but he doesn't drink. He smokes a lot, but I don't mind that. By the way, I enrolled in a nursing course to become a certified nurse in about twelve months. As you know, right now I am only a Red Cross nurse. Willi will do the same."

"Sounds good," Muttchen said. "Let us know when you are going to have your wedding."

My foster mother was somewhat cool about the news. I knew she didn't agree with my mother, not the way she behaved anyway, but it was so very typical of her.

My mother had the abortion and then got married on June 4th, 1947.

I didn't like Uncle Willi, as I had to call him. Not only was he not the nicest-looking man, but I found him clumsy. He was the same height as my mother and seemed not too friendly but rather dour.

A Penny Always Has Two Sides | 231

Anyway, my mother said he was good to her. He didn't drink and at least she didn't have to be afraid that he would sleep around like Richard did.

After they got married my mother didn't show up much again and when she did, she constantly criticized me. I couldn't do anything good enough in her eyes and I felt unworthy in her presence. She gave me a complex that I didn't lose for the longest time.

She went to my teacher to check how I was doing in school and made my teacher suspicious of my life at home.

I was in grade five by then and had a very good and kind teacher. I actually had her for almost three years, until grade eight. I knew, right from the beginning, I could talk to her about almost everything.

After my mother left that day, Frau Gebhard talked to me about the interview she had had with her and I had to fill her in a bit about why I lived with my foster mother and that I was happy there as long I didn't see my mother. Frau Gebhard was puzzled and I explained to her why I was so scared of my mother. I realized that I shouldn't have told her about it, but I trusted her and, from that day on, I believed that I had two people who would protect me, Muttchen and Frau Gebhard.

My mother demanded that I come to visit her and Uncle Willi at least once a month. I hated these visits, but Muttchen made me go. She said, "You must go, it is your mother and she has a right to see you." I argued that she could come to visit us. Muttchen, however, told me to do what I was told to do and so I went to see them, always afraid that, in my mother's eyes, I would do something wrong. Often she told me that she knew I didn't love her, only my Muttchen. And she was right, but I didn't want to hurt her, so I never said anything.

One day my mother was home, sick with her leg, and was playing the piano. I actually still loved it when she played and so I was standing beside her and watched and listened when she suggested that I should take lessons. I kind of liked the idea and so I agreed. She told me that she would pay for the lessons but I had to promise to come every day to practice and, again, I agreed to that too.

She enrolled me at the same music school she went to during the war and I still knew the teacher, Fräulein Bruening. I was sad to hear that her mother, who taught me how to knit, had passed away a year earlier.

So I didn't feel strange when I went and at first had fun. The everyday practice, however, didn't work out all the time, since both my mother and my stepfather worked different shifts. Sometimes Willi or my mother was home and had to sleep during the day and I wasn't able to practice. So I didn't make the progress my mother hoped for but she blamed that on me. When I mentioned that I was not able to practice because I didn't want to wake her or Uncle Willi up, she was upset and told me that this was just an excuse; I should have come at different times to fit in with their schedule. Well, the whole idea of practicing was not going well at all.

One day Muttchen called me while I was playing outside to go to practice and without much washing up, I went.

To my surprise, my mother was home and when I came in she told me that she had changed her shift so that she could listen to my progress. I didn't like that much but there was no way out and needless to say, it didn't go well at all. It made me nervous that she stood beside me and later started to count the beat, 1 2 3 4, 1 2 3 4, etc., with a little stick to get me going. It made me so nervous that I made more and more mistakes and I felt that I couldn't lift my fingers anymore; they seemed to stick to the keyboard. I started to cry and told her I couldn't practice with her standing beside me. She looked at me with that mean look and then, suddenly, I knew what was coming.

She asked to see my fingers and then she screamed, "How dare you touch my piano with those dirty fingernails!" And she hit my fingers with her stick. And she continued, "Don't tell me you ever practiced at all, your playing sounds awful. I can see that I am spending my money for your lessons for nothing. You are a nuisance, a no-good, you always were and it will never change." And then it came. She took the music book and hit me and hit me and I fell under the piano and she pulled me up by my hair and hit me more and more until I came loose from her grip and ran. I ran out, down the stairs, fell, got up and ran all the way home to Muttchen. I cried and cried and when I was finally in her arms I sobbed even more. She looked at me and her face was so sad, but she waited until I was able to speak.

She was very upset when she heard that it was my mother and not, as she assumed at first, a fight or something I had gotten into.

She cleaned my face and saw all the bruises that were starting to develop. And then she said, "I will call Children's Aid."

She left to go to the grocers, which was located at the corner of our street, to make the phone call.

When she returned her face was harsh and she said, "We have an appointment within an hour and we should leave at once." We were within walking distance and arrived on time. I was scared since I remembered what my mother always said, "If you don't do what I tell you to do, I will make sure you will be sent to reform school."

I told my Muttchen about my fear and she assured me that I had done nothing wrong. "Don't be afraid. You ran out because she was not herself when she hit you."

I argued, "I didn't clean up properly. My fingernails were dirty."

But Muttchen waved me off and said, "Clean up with what? She knows we have no soap, not even warm water. Don't worry, you did nothing wrong. The only thing you did was not be able to play the piano under pressure."

We arrived at the partly bombed building and we didn't have to wait long. We walked through a hallway and knocked at the door of an office. After waiting a second or so we were asked to step in and told to sit down since the person who had our file was still with another person. And while we waited for about ten minutes my heart almost came out of my throat. I was so afraid that I would have to go back to my mother or to reform school because I had run away from her. I told myself, I shouldn't have done it, I shouldn't have done it.

Muttchen calmed me down again and then a friendly older man entered the room and sat down behind the large desk. He looked first at Muttchen and then he turned his face to me, opened the big file he brought with him, and then with a friendly smile asked me what had happened to me and why my face was so swollen.

I looked at Muttchen and started to sob but she just stroked my hair and gently said, "Tell him. Nothing will happen to you, you are safe here."

And so I started talking. At first with hesitation but after I realized that nothing bad would happen to me, I told them all of it and after I was finished I started to cry uncontrollably.

The man still looked friendly, came around to me and he too stroked my hair and asked me with a very soft voice to go out into the hall because he had to talk to my foster mother in private. I looked at my foster mother. I didn't want to leave and with more tears I asked if I would have to go to reform school. The man looked at me and asked me who had given me that idea and I told him that my mother always told me that would happen to me if I were bad. But Muttchen reassured me again that nothing like that would happen, not now, not ever. "Just wait for me in the hall."

And so I went, sitting on the bench we had sat on before, still afraid and skeptical, seeing myself in reform school, whatever that was, or worse yet, going back to my mother. It was like a nightmare. And then I prayed, "God, please let me stay with my Muttchen, please!"

Muttchen came out after about fifteen minutes and reassured me, "Everything will be fine, Steffchen." She explained, "At the moment you cannot go for practice anymore, do you mind?"

And I answered, "I would rather quit the lessons altogether."

"We will see," and again, "We will see. Your mother probably will want to stop paying for the lessons anyway. Your guardian will talk to her. He will let us know. Don't worry, everything will be fine."

A month or so later, Muttchen received a registered letter from Children's Aid informing her that the state had taken full custody of me and she, Meta Pech, became my legal foster mother. I would stay with her until the case was reviewed in January 1949, when I would become thirteen years old and would be allowed to decide if I wanted to stay with my foster mother or would like to return and live with my birth mother. My mother had the right to see me at any time if she wished to do so. They ordered that for the first year, Muttchen and I had to report every three months to my now legally appointed guardian and they told Muttchen that the department had sent a copy of this letter to my school.

A few days later my mother came to visit. She brought my new stepfather as well and over a cup of coffee my mother expressed her concern that my Muttchen had gone straight to Children's Aid. She admitted to Muttchen that, yes, she had been upset with me and she shouldn't have lost it. "But why did you have to go to the authorities right away, Meta?"

"I'll tell you why, Rosi, because of the state Steffchen was in. You don't hit a child like that. I realize that she probably was not too clean and all that, but to hit her like you did was unacceptable. I understand you have done that to her before, when she was much younger?"

"Did she tell you that, Meta?" and turning to me, "Did you, Steffie?"

"Yes, Mutti, I did," I answered.

My stepfather looked at me and said, "You liar!" But my mother waved him off.

"Willi, don't mix yourself in with this, the conversation is between Meta and myself."

He looked at her somehow disappointed, shaking his

head, and answered, "You don't have to take this shit from an eleven-year-old child."

But again she said, "Please keep out of it, Willi."

Anyway, Rosi continued to say to my foster mother, "Now you have almost everything you wanted, don't you? But I tell you, please don't ever come to me to talk about adoption. I will not give her up. I will never give her to you because that is what you want, to have her for yourself. Well, it will not happen."

My mother looked at my foster mother with a face I knew very well and I was frightened, but Muttchen didn't care, she just shook her head and asked her, "Rosi, why did you change to be like the old times again? I hate to say this, but I hope you don't forget how you knocked at my door not even two years back. And to answer your question, I want what is good for Steffie, and obviously you, her birth mother, are not the best example to give her what she needs most, namely, love. I have the feeling that you don't even know the meaning of the word."

My mother was furious now. "You had to mention my cry for help, didn't you, but since it has come up again I will tell you once more that I am sorry and, yes, I will never forget what you did for us. You were good to us, but this is another matter, Meta, this has nothing to do with what happened then. I am talking about what happened now."

She turned to Willi and said, "Let's go." While putting her coat on she turned to me, "From now on, I want you to see me every month. We will make a schedule. And by the way, I will not be paying for your piano lessons any longer." And with that they left.

Muttchen got up, too. She had tears in her eyes, something I almost never saw. Slowly she came to me and took me in her so-protective arms and we both cried until we could no longer and then we laughed, a happy laugh, and we were thankful that everything would be better from now on.

We made do with what we had

Muttchen's health was not the best, but we were still happy.

I helped her keep the fire going and look after the wood. Spring came early and since the summer was warm, her little parcel of land gave us enough vegetables and fruit for the winter.

She still went a lot to the black market but because her brother from Weissensee/Malchow (in the east sector of Berlin), who had two pigs and chickens, often brought eggs and meat to us, we had things to exchange most of the time.

Also, Muttchen had relatives in Magdeburg and if we were really short on something that we could not get elsewhere, she would take the train and visit these people. I had never met them but Muttchen told me they were very helpful and became rich because they had a big farm and exchanged food for anything they could get. Muttchen said if this continued they would have carpets for their cows soon.

Anyway, Muttchen went there only if she was in need

and because they would tell her where she could find other farmers who were looking for goods in exchange for different food or clothes, etc.

The only danger was to come back through the border control where the Russian soldiers could confiscate everything people had in their suitcases, knapsacks, etc., in other words you would come home empty-handed. And that was not the worst that could happen; they also put people into jail, sometimes for days.

Muttchen got caught twice. She lost everything she had in her bags and was thrown into jail.

These were times when I was so helpless and my fear of losing her was indescribable. I used to be alone for days, but our neighbours were always there for me and helped me to believe through their words and comforting that she would come back. And when she finally returned I always said, "Thank you, God."

So the end of 1947 and the beginning of 1948 were not too bad. We had some food and a warm room. The only thing missing was still the steady electricity. But we now had more hours of it and were used to the interruptions.

My school work was back on track again and most of the time I shared class best with one of my three girl-friends. Reni was constantly in competition with me and competing was fun. But still, the four of us, Astrid, Christa, Reni, and I, were inseparable and were called the clover leaf.

We sure had good times, but also bad times too because we sometimes got in trouble. My shyness disappeared when I was with them and the little devil in me came out more often than I wished.

If we did something very bad, Muttchen had to come to

school because Frau Gebhard knew that I was the one who had the ideas that got the four of us into trouble; the other three were just happy following me. During these meetings Muttchen would always find excuses for me, but as soon I came home, she would punish me by not talking to me anymore. I became air to her; she didn't see me at all.

For me this was the worst punishment I could think of. I would have preferred that she hit me, but she never did, she wouldn't even raise her voice. It was awful. And the worst thing, on top of this dilemma, was that I developed a stubborn streak. It took me the longest time to say, "I am sorry," the only words she was waiting for and expected.

The hormonal changes in my body didn't help either. I started to get mouthy and the bathroom mirror was mine for hours.

I developed so quickly that my body got beyond me. My mood swings were overwhelming and I am sure Muttchen didn't know what to do with me at times.

Because of these developments it took only a short time until I looked much older than I was and therefore many people expected so much more from me than I could deliver. When I turned twelve everybody said, "You look like you are fifteen." I thought this was great but my foster mother was worried.

As well, I grew out of everything I had in the way of clothing. Muttchen still had some curtains which became two beautiful dresses but I needed new shoes, a winter coat, and a bra and underwear, things one could only buy on the black market. Both of us had to go since I needed to try on these items.

The very first time Muttchen took me there, it was an

experience I would never forget. The people who had the items we needed so desperately were not standing openly on the street and it certainly was not like the market I always believed it would be. Men and women offered their merchandise in hidden places. They were standing in alleys, in door entrances, or behind a corner. Their faces were hidden and whatever one wanted to buy or exchange was under their coats or in old bags and the like. And they were always ready to run from the police. We, too, had to be ready to run because it didn't matter, buyers or sellers, everybody would be punished for being there. But nobody cared, the black market was a necessity; we all needed such a market in these times. From it some got rich and some of us stayed very poor.

Muttchen knew her way around. She asked a few questions and was directed to the right people who might have the items she was asking for. But to try on clothes was another story. We managed to get a coat, a second-hand pair of shoes, and a pair of pants for me. I hated all of them! Muttchen, though, was happy that we at least got something and told me to smarten up. So whether I wanted to or not, I had to wear the clothes. We couldn't find a bra so I had to go without one. I was embarrassed when these things wiggled around, so in school I held my arms to my chest so that nobody could see my ever so rapidly growing boobs.

My foster mother explained to me that I would get my period soon. When I heard that I would bleed, I panicked right away. I saw the pictures in my head of when my mother was raped and blood was running down her legs.

Muttchen tried everything possible to make clear to me that every girl would have these monthly bleedings sooner or later. She partially explained the facts of life to me, which I didn't want to hear. I was terrified of what would happen to me.

A bit later she told me that she bought some pads which a neighbour made from a bed sheet. I looked at her and then down to the pads and told her I didn't need them. "I will never bleed."

She smiled and said, "But just in case, I will put them in your drawer and when you need them, then you have them. But let me know. Remember, there is nothing wrong with it."

Things are looking up

We still had some people coming to warm themselves, but the numbers started to decrease as they, too, now had their own little pipe stove installed and no longer needed to warm up at our place. We got rid of the movie seats we had in our living room and made them into firewood. We also got some furniture from the shelter where it was still stored and had not been used for firewood, as originally planned. It all looked very poor, but we were happy that we were more or less on our own again.

We celebrated Muttchen's 60th birthday. All the neighbours and Muttchen's relatives came and we had a good time. Everybody brought something to eat and to drink; the men started to have a few too many drinks but who cared? There was laughter, and we even danced.

I knew by now how to celebrate everything that was worth celebrating. In Muttchen's house there was always more laughter than tears and I, myself, was happy and started to lose some of my fear of having to go back to my mother. Muttchen gave me the confidence to believe in myself, which my mother always tried to take away from me. And by giving me some responsibilities she helped me to lift my head high.

I was, by the way, responsible for taking care of the wood for our stove. Since we always played in the ruins, I collected wood wherever I could. As a matter of fact, since I was the only girl on the block, the boys helped me and I helped them, and in a way I became a little bit like a tomboy.

Once we saw a big four-by-six beam sticking out of part of what used to be a bathroom on the fourth floor. We climbed up and one of the boys told me to climb in the still-hanging bath tub to reach the beam. We took a handsaw with us and I was supposed to saw the thing down. They told me to be careful, but since I was relatively light I could not foresee a problem. This beam was so big we would all get some wood. Anyway I climbed into the bathtub and started to work on it and all went well...until I heard a big crack and then I fell with that bathtub and part of the beam straight down and landed just by luck onto the second floor. I didn't fall down to the ground but only to the second floor and hung from an iron beam, like hanging on a thread. I was not hurt but started to shake because I knew I could fall further. The boys screamed to me not to move and tried to reach me by climbing down to me, but then what? I didn't have to think further because the bathtub started moving and I fell to the ground floor. The miracle was that I was not hurt much. I had some bruises on my arms and my bum was purple, but other than that I was fine, and we had the beam too. It fell down a bit later, right into the bathtub, just a second after I had cleared it. One of the boys said, "Tell your mother you don't need a bath today, because you just had one." We all laughed and left after we shared the big beam, which luckily had come down without killing me.

Muttchen was so happy when I came with the wood but I never told her how I got it.

As agreed, I had to visit my mother and my stepfather every month. My mother still criticized me more or less for everything I did or did not do but I didn't care as much as before, except when Willi mixed in. I hated him. My mother tried to bring us together but I told her straight out that I wanted nothing to do with him. And so our relationship was not the best.

Once I asked her if I could see Richard, my first stepfather, and she almost slapped me for it. I never mentioned him again.

I also asked her why they never came to visit us. I said, "Muttchen would probably love to see you. You didn't even come to her birthday. You know, she waited."

My mother answered, "You are just saying that. She would probably slam the door in our faces and you would love it."

"No, she wouldn't. She would never do that. All you have to say is that you are sorry for what you said to her."

"Yes, maybe I should," my mother mumbled, "but I still will not give you to her." And again she said, "I'm sorry, but I will not give you up, but I should have told her that in a different way."

I then realized that my mother was sorry for what she had said to her when they had the big argument. So I looked right at her and said, "Muttchen would never slam the door in your face. You know she forgives everything. Just come. You will see."

I just hoped she would apologize to my Muttchen, so

I invited her without asking my foster mother or really knowing that Muttchen wouldn't slam the door in their faces. But when my mother and Willi came, Muttchen asked them in and even though my mother didn't apologize, they talked a bit and I guess this made them both feel better.

At the beginning of June my mother came to tell us that she was expecting a baby in January. We were both surprised because not too long before she had had the abortion.

Muttchen mentioned that to her and my mother replied, "My legs are a bit better and the doctor says that I must rest a lot. At the moment I feel fine. The other pregnancy wasn't right from the beginning. So, we will see."

"How do you rest when you are working? You are still working, aren't you?"

"Yes, I am, but if my legs get worse again, I will have to stop for a while. Willi would like to have this baby. I will worry about it when I have to."

Muttchen said nothing, what could she say anyway? As she said later, it was none of her business. But I knew she couldn't understand my mother.

In a way I was happy to have a brother or a sister. I told Muttchen that I would pick up the baby and bring it to our house and we could cuddle it together. But Muttchen just smiled and told me there was a bit more to it than just cuddling the baby. "And anyway, Rosi probably won't allow you to bring the baby to our place often."

The Blockade

From the beginning of May until July of 1945 the Soviets, who had conquered Berlin, were the only Allied force to occupy and provisionally govern the city.

In June, before the Western Allies took over their sectors, the Soviets allowed the formation of several German parties in their occupied zone and in Berlin. In April 1946, following the wishes of the Soviets, the Communist Party (KPD) and the Social Party (SPD) were combined into one communist party, the SED. Only in Berlin, after a referendum by the Berliner people, were both parties, the SED and the SPD, allowed.

Former German members of the communist party, who under Hitler's regime had been sent to prison, returned from concentration camps and jails and were granted many important government positions from the Soviets. With that, all of the East Zone and of Berlin was more or less governed by communists.

At first the Western Allies, who moved into their sectors in July and August, agreed to what was already in place, thereby giving up their veto to the Soviets. This also made it difficult for them to make changes in the future. But the Western Allies realized more and more that the agreements that had been made were not working. And even though they tried to achieve a compromise, they realized how hard it was to work in unity with the Soviets.

The headquarters of the four Allies was located in the East of Berlin and this already created friction for the Western Allies. The Soviets' check-points included their allies and had a very strict and stressful protocol. All decisions that were made had to be unanimous, otherwise the Soviets would use their veto to force an agreement that would be then in their favour.

The real political strain started on October 20th,, 1946, when the first and last free election took place and when more or less all Berliners voted for the SPD. In 1947, when leaders of the SPD voted for a mayor for all Berlin, the Soviets vetoed the decision. The Western Allies tried to negotiate but without success and the Cold War between the West and the East threw its first shadow over the city.

Also, to make it easier on the recovery of the German economy and the rebuilding of the country, all Allies suggested a new common currency, but the Soviets set out rules that were unacceptable to the West.

And so it went until the East and the West separated completely and within a short time both parts had their own currency and economic policies. Although the Soviets lost control over West Berlin, they controlled all direct passages to and from Berlin without having to go through the West at all, and the East part, which was now a communist state, became the biggest impasse between the East and the West. The Soviets closed off all routes to and from the West zones, including all waterways from the West sectors.

West Berlin again was without electricity, gas, and food. And with that, on June 24, 1948, the blockade began.

Most West Berliners, including my Muttchen, were glued to their radios. And yet I don't think that many people, and certainly not I, understood what was happening to us. This new page in history was in effect, one of the cruelest attempts ever made to starve an entire population.

Everything started to feel like the first days after the war. Before the blockade Berlin was still lacking every little necessity of a normal life because we were still surrounded by rubble, but now, after only a week or so, we had absolutely nothing. Again!

Two days after the blockade had begun, however, the Western Allies started the largest airlift ever known to date. The effort to help was like a wonder sent by God. We wouldn't have survived otherwise.

When the planes started flying over West Berlin, they came about every two minutes and it was like music to our ears. The effort to save and protect us from total starvation was indescribable.

Of course, the American soldiers had no shortage of German "sweethearts". Not only were the soldiers clean looking, but many were kind and some provided food for the whole family. The girls were looked down on by others, but most didn't care. We were all so hungry that every young girl over sixteen ran into a soldier's arms if she could find one.

I mentioned once to Muttchen that I found it very "chic" to have a soldier as a boyfriend. When she realized that I meant it, she naturally almost flipped. I didn't know why, but I never mentioned the possibility again.

Not long after the blockade had started, all children received warm soup at school. They weren't the greatest kinds of soup but it was a warm meal. Once a week each class had to volunteer three or four pupils to help with the distribution and later with the clean-up, and for us kids it was the greatest thing to be called up to help for one or even two days.

We felt very important on these occasions because not only could we stand behind these big canisters and give everybody a ladle of soup but we could give some more if it was a friend or a well-liked kid. Of course we were not supposed to do this, but everybody did. Also we, the helpers, were allowed to take some soup home to our parents, which for them was a welcome meal as well. Most everybody's favourite soup was a cookie soup. It was delicious, made from cookie crumbs; I can still taste it.

Once a month we also received a little chocolate bar. I never ate mine, but would save it to share it with Muttchen. Muttchen, of course, wouldn't eat her half but saved it for me for another day. I always pretended that I didn't want it but naturally took it anyway.

Our ration cards were not shortened, but when you wanted to get something from the store it was not available and therefore the ration cards were for the birds at times.

Talking about birds, again I caught sparrows; five little birds made a good soup. Muttchen had the honour of plucking them. We both felt sorry for the birds, but our stomachs didn't.

Muttchen was back to the black market, which still flourished, but she did not have much left to exchange for goods or money to buy things with. We were hungry most of the time and cold even though we still had our little stove in the living room. We had to conserve because we didn't know when the misery would stop.

We lived from day to day and hunger was now a sickness everybody had to live with. Unless of course you had money, which meant the new West Mark, which was worth much more than the East Mark. But we had neither. The little money Muttchen received wasn't enough to take away our ever-increasing hunger.

So again, we had to exchange goods for goods or pay outrageous amounts to get anything. Well, Muttchen almost ran out of goods and so we very often went to bed hungry. To overcome the feeling of hunger and despair of sitting in the dark, we would often go to bed very early and we would sing. Muttchen had a wonderful voice and so did I actually and when we were singing, we were happy together and forgot our misery.

One day I came home from school and told my foster mother that the Americans threw chocolate bars down from their airplanes. Muttchen didn't believe me, but I told her it was true; all I had to do was walk to the airport in Tempelhof.

Of course the airport was too far away to walk, but by streetcar it was possible. Most of the time the streetcars would come on time and so it was worth a try.

Muttchen was skeptical but let me go anyway. The first day was unsuccessful but I could tell her that it really was true; the little bars came down via little parachutes made out of handkerchiefs or other materials.

"Muttchen, I even saw the people who threw them out of the plane!" God, I was so excited, I wanted to scream!

She laughed and was happy for me and I asked right away, "Can I go again, please, even if I don't get anything, at least I can watch. Please let me go!"

She argued that I should do my homework first. But by that time it would be dark, so after one more "Please," she agreed but warned me right away, "But then no more." And so I went and believe it or not, I got a little bar of chocolate. I couldn't believe my luck because so many children waved to the airplanes, which came very punctually every two minutes.

I saw the pilot and the crew and I was a lucky one who caught a chocolate bar. Later I learned that not all planes threw chocolate, some threw packs of chewing gum down, which was even more precious because gum would last longer.

When a new plane came we would all run to the lowest point before the landing because that was where the parachutes usually fell to the ground. The most amazing part was that these people, who had fun seeing us run to get a goody, were rescuing our city from starvation. When I think about it now, it was almost an impossible task, but they did it and I was there and will never forget what they did for us. What an accomplishment!

In January I celebrated my 13th birthday and even though we had nothing much to eat, I could invite my girlfriends and Muttchen served gruel with conserved blueberries. It was a feast.

On January 31st, 1949, my half-brother Martin was born and I helped him come into this terrible world where we had no hope of ever getting out of our misery.

Muttchen did whatever she could to make ends meet, but it was hard. Again we had people sitting in our living room because we still had some coal and wood, but we didn't know if it would carry us through the winter.

My schoolwork was good but could have been better if I had put more effort into it. Actually we were all not very interested in school anymore. Everybody became depressed. The only thing that kept us going was the hope that this would all end soon.

Due to being undernourished I started to have problems with my teeth and so I had to see a dentist. His name was Dr. Hund (Dr. Dog). What a name, but since the pain became worse and this was the only dentist who was still around, I had to go to him.

He had a look, gave me a needle, and told me to wait in the waiting room, which I did. However, a bit later, the pain was gone and so I went home. When I told Muttchen about it, she was very angry but then she laughed because in a way it was funny. I would have liked to have seen his face when he realized that I had gone home. I was able to make it for months without seeing him again. However when I had to go back, you can imagine that he gave me an earful and this time I had to wait in his only chair until he could fill the tooth. I still have the filling and many more from that time.

I had become quite pretty by now but I thought myself ugly, and when we had a garden fest during late spring of 1949, right smack among the ruins in our courtyard, I didn't want to go because I had nothing nice to wear. Again Muttchen found some material on the black market and a friend and dressmaker of hers made a pretty dress for me.

I stood in front of our mirror for hours, but even the

new dress didn't change my face and I wondered why many people whispered that I had become very pretty.

My mother, Willi, and little baby Martin were also there. When my mother saw that I had a new dress, she told Meta right away that she was spoiling me too much. But Muttchen just laughed and told her that right now I was her only sunshine.

The Soviets realized that they couldn't break the spirit of the Allies and the West Berliners. They hadn't calculated on the toughness of the Berliners, who, with the help of the Americans, the British, and the French, could withstand the evil with which the Soviets tried to break the people's will to live.

And so, after all together 213,000 flights and 1.7 million tons of provisions, including coal, and a bit later, even a whole power station that was brought in piece by piece and assembled in Berlin, on May 24th, 1949, the blockade came to an end and West Berlin came to life again.

It was like a wonder. Suddenly the stores were full of goods, goods I had never seen before or tasted. A banana, for example, was a fruit I hadn't known. I saw it for the first time in a vegetable store and again later when my mother gave one to my brother. I wanted to taste it, but my mother told me that I would have to wait since they were very expensive.

Later, when I came home to my Muttchen and told her that I wanted a banana and my mother told me I had to wait because they were too expensive, she went to the store right away and bought several for me. They tasted like a field of flowers. I loved them.

Astrid's mother opened a variety store right beside a vegetable store. The fruits there always looked so inviting and I could have eaten the whole store empty, but of course we hardly had the money to buy anything. So at night, after the stores closed, my girlfriends and I had a ball going through the garbage to look for the fruits and vegetables that were thrown out because they were not fresh anymore or were half spoiled. We sorted almost everything out and took home whatever was still edible. The oranges were the best I had ever had and I couldn't get enough of them.

Time flew. Unfortunately my mother became sick again and after she was admitted to the hospital, I had to baby-sit my half-brother. This of course spoiled my summer, but Muttchen told me it was my duty to help my mother. And honestly I loved my little half-brother.

I was with my brother for almost three months and by the time my mother came back home, he didn't want to go to her anymore. She was disappointed and it was hard for her, but I guess children love the person who cares for them.

My teenage years

School in the meantime had already started and when I returned Frau Gebhard had taken over another grade and was not our teacher anymore. We had had her for almost three years and she was more a mother than a teacher to us. We would have done anything for her because she was kind and, especially to me, she was like a good friend. Oh, how we all missed her.

But that was not the worst of it; about three months later we had to move to another, newly built school and there again we had a new teacher. The four of us made up our minds in approximately one minute that we didn't like the new teacher and sure enough we never did. It was unfair but we compared her with Frau Gebhard and she wasn't her. She was definitely only a teacher and had no patience with any of us. All our classmates agreed except one girl whom we called "arse licker", a not very nice thing to say but that was how we all felt. The class average dropped dramatically.

Reni and I became so bad in school that we almost failed. My mother fumed, but I couldn't have cared less and I became quite defiant.

Even my foster mother couldn't understand what was

wrong with me and I guess nobody realized that I had become depressed and this was how I reacted.

My three girlfriends were my only haven and we stuck together like glue.

Soon we started confirmation classes together and we didn't like the confirmation teacher who taught us either. He was old and spat when he talked. Since we had to sit in the front row (as a precaution because he didn't trust us), it was not very pleasant. So one day I brought an umbrella to class and when he started talking and spitting again, I opened the umbrella. I was thrown out of class faster than I could close the umbrella. It was approximately a month before the confirmation was scheduled when Muttchen received the letter from the church that the pastor would not confirm me because of bad behaviour.

I had to tell Muttchen what happened and she was livid. Since confirmation was very celebrated in Germany with many guests being invited, Muttchen went with me to another church and after a big discussion and a lot of charm, which Muttchen always showed when she wanted something special, the other pastor agreed to confirm me. I saw in his eyes that somehow he was amused by all of this, but of course he couldn't say it and so he warned me that this was my last chance.

"Smarten up, girl. Pretty soon you will be a lady, so behave like one. From what I have heard about you, I think it will take a lot of practice." He smiled and continued, "But you can do it, I know you can." And with that, he was in my heart and I guess in Muttchen's too, because my Muttchen never gave up on me.

I told my girlfriends about how nice the new pastor was and they said right away, "We must be confirmed together." So they spoke to their mothers, who understood the problem, and spoke to the pastor as well. After they explained the situation, he agreed and, miraculously, we were confirmed together as originally planned.

We were confirmed in groups of four and the four of us made sure we were standing so that our initials would spell "ARSCH" which translated meant arse, Astrid, Reni, Steffie and Christa. ("Ch" was never divided in the German language.) It was sad to say that even in church we did not have much respect, but that was what the four of us were like at fourteen.

For everybody it was a special day, except for me. I was ashamed of my shoes. I had to wear these old-fashioned terrible-looking shoes, tie-ups with a half-inch-high, wide, big heel. Nurses or old women might wear them, but not me; I wanted pumps like many wore for the occasion.

Muttchen bought a really nice dress for me but my mother committed to the shoes. And so I got these ugly black walking shoes. Ugly! But my Muttchen told me to wear them because they were from my mother.

I wanted to become a nurse but since I was too young and didn't want to continue high school it was suggested that I first take a one-year course that combined a household year and school, and after that I would be accepted into nursing college. After my mother told me that this was the best way to get into nursing, I agreed, and was accepted as an apprentice to work for a family of three.

After working there for about three months, I realized that I was more or less fulfilling the function of a cheap maid; the money I made for the work I had to do was peanuts. I had to work almost ten hours a day with only every second Sunday off.

I went to my foster mother and complained bitterly but she had no sympathy at all and I learned quickly that failure or giving up was not in the cards. She told me straight out that I had better finish the year or else.

But the longer I stayed, the longer the year became and I realized that I was not good at serving people or becoming a nurse either where I would have to cater not only to the people's welfare but also clean around their beds, push bed-pans, etc. At least that's how it was in the '50s.

I must have been not too bad at my job, though, because the lady asked me shortly before I finished the year if I cared to stay. The "no" came out of my mouth faster than my brain could work and so I returned home and had no job.

Muttchen, at this time, had rented out our little bed-room to a woman named Frau Moritz. She did it shortly before I returned home because, as she explained, we needed the money and could share the space for a while until Frau Moritz could find a little place of her own. But since there was still a shortage of housing, I knew this could mean years. And so now Muttchen slept on a little convertible easy-chair and I had the front sofa. I felt our privacy was gone and it added to my uncomfortable feeling of not really belonging anywhere.

West Berlin started to rebuild again in earnest and by 1952 you could see that progress was being made. At least we had electricity, gas, and water again. Our little pipe stove had been thrown out and we were promised that come winter we would have central heating again.

The only thing we really didn't have were jobs. Due to many political complications the jobless figure fell from 309,000 in 1950 to under 100,000 in 1957, so for me, the chances of getting a job without a proper education were almost zero.

My foster mother told me that I should have stayed with the family I did my household year with or gone on to be a nurse. She couldn't understand that I didn't want to be what I had learned to hate, serving other people, and cleaning and cooking for them.

But she couldn't say that I didn't try to get a job and one day I came home and told her that I was starting in a sport store as a sales clerk apprentice. We had to go to see my guardian and sign some papers and after that I had a job with little pay, but at least I was working, and I had to go to school again, twice a week, for three years.

From the beginning, I liked my job and I had much success dealing with customers and bringing in business, and customers came back because of the good service they received from me. Some even said they were coming back because of my smile. I was flattered.

And the owners were pleased with me too. I liked going to school and Muttchen was glad that I seemed to be happy.

This went on until one day my boss's wife brought in their seven-year-old son and asked me to baby-sit, which I did of course, but after several weeks I felt this was not right. I didn't say anything for a while, but I was peeved. My foster mother didn't know about my new problem. I dared not complain, but in school my class teacher noticed because my performance had gone down. She asked me if everything was all right but I said it was fine and I would try to improve.

My private life was great. My girlfriends were happy for me that I had found an apprenticeship, which was hard to come by. When we got together we still giggled a lot and talked about boys and even the boyfriends that none of us had. It was an unfamiliar subject for us until Reni, who had problems with one of her eyes (a birth defect), needed surgery. Her parents found a famous doctor in Dresden, where her family originally came from, and so she went back to Dresden for a month or so.

When she returned, we didn't notice her eye patch as much as how she had changed to a softer Reni than the one we were familiar with. We questioned her about it and with a big smile she told us that she was in love with the surgeon.

"In love? How come, did he kiss you?"

But she said, "No, we just flirted and I think he is in love with me, too." Well, we were all jealous and thought of nothing else than to fall in love ourselves, hopefully sooner than later.

I told Muttchen about Reni's love affair and even though she laughed, we talked about it seriously and she warned me that falling in love could be dangerous at our age and I should make sure, that if it happened to me, whoever it was would not take advantage.

"Why?" I asked. "I don't understand. Why would somebody take advantage of me if he loves me?"

"Well," she said, "Young men sometimes want more than falling in love. Just be careful and don't let anyone touch you." And with that our conversation ended.

I told Reni about the talk I had had with my foster mother and she shook her head, "That is nonsense. Why would someone take advantage of you if you are both in love with each other? You silly goose, don't talk to your foster mother about things like that. Grown-ups always think they know everything."

And so I didn't talk to Muttchen about love anymore. What a mistake!

Am I falling in love?

ONE DAY I SERVED AN OLDER-LOOKING GENTLEMAN, A CUS-tomer who couldn't take his eyes off me and made me uncomfortable but not really in a bad way. After he left, I kind of thought about him for a while, something I hadn't done before.

He came back a few weeks later, bought something again, and asked me what my name was and told me how pretty I was. I looked at him and wondered why a cus-tomer would tell me that I was pretty. From my point of view, he, himself, was not good looking. He was too old, but on the other hand, he was very kind and seemed interesting.

Later, as he was going out of the door he turned and asked if I had had lunch yet and if not could he take me out for lunch or at least for a coffee.

I was surprised but answered, "I brought my lunch with me and there is no café around here anyway."

He smiled and said, "Perhaps another time," and left.

I didn't see him again until one day, when I was walking home, a car stopped beside me. And when I looked to see why the car stopped I recognized the driver as the customer who had invited me for lunch. He rolled the window down and, smiling, said, "Steffie, isn't it?" He remembered! And a moment later he asked if I needed a ride home. Since I still had about thirty minutes to walk, I didn't object and slipped into the car.

He looked at me, smiling his charming smile, but I felt uncomfortable. He asked me where I lived and when I told him, he said he knew where it was.

We didn't talk much, because I was shy and was glad when he stopped in front of our apartment building. I thanked him and got out of the car quickly because I didn't want my foster mother, or, worse, a neighbour to see me. And he just said, "I hope to see you again soon," and drove on. His name was Kurt.

I didn't mention any of this to my foster mother but had long talks with my girlfriends about it. They thought this was the greatest adventure I could ever experience. Reni even asked me if we had kissed yet and I, of course, answered that he was much too old for me and I never would kiss him because my foster mother would not approve.

"Remember, Reni, she told me to be careful with men."

Reni however thought nothing of it. "Steffie, if you find him nice you could kiss him. Since he is older he would never take advantage of you. By the way how old is he?"

"I don't know, but maybe as old as my first stepfather was," I answered.

Reni thought about this for a while and with a smile she said, "I guess that is old then?" She continued, saying, "Is he good looking?"

And I had to say, "No, not really, but he is nice to talk to and he listens. And by the way he is not my boyfriend.

He is just a nice man and I like him very much. He is almost like my first stepfather was; he is just nice to me, that's all."

Since Reni lived closer to me than Astrid and Christa, we got together more often and considered ourselves "super" best friends. When we got together the first thing we would talk about was boys.

Reni's eye, by the way, didn't turn out the way she and her family had hoped, and she told me she had to go back for a second surgery. I found this very bad, but she loved the idea because she still dreamed of her doctor. When I asked her how old he was, she answered that he was older, but very good-looking. "Oh, how I love him!" she cried out.

Another girl, Marleen, whom I knew and who lived close to me as well, came over one day and asked me if I felt like going to a dance with her. Since I had never been to a dance, I said that I would have to ask my foster mother. Marleen suggested that I not mention a dance but say instead that I would be with her and we might go window-shopping.

But I was not too sure since we would probably be home later than my curfew time, which was 11:00 pm.

Anyway I told Muttchen I was going with Marleen. I would be home early because we were only going window-shopping. Muttchen told me to have fun and so after I dressed and put on a bit make-up, I sneaked out. Make-up was a no-no for my Muttchen.

We went to a place called "Resi", a large dancing establishment with a big band playing. I thought this was only possible at concerts. The place was huge and in my eyes, marvelous. The most incredible thing was that every table had a phone and pneumatic tube–conveyed mail. Unbelievable!

I whispered, "How do we get in here?" We were not eighteen yet.

But Marleen told me not to worry, she knew somebody, and we would have no problems. "The only thing we have to watch is when the police come. We have to go straight to the washrooms and wait until they are gone again. Don't worry, Steffie, I have been here several times, nothing will happen."

We made it in, thanks to Marleen's connections, and found a small table. We ordered two Cokes and when the waitress asked us if we meant rum and Coke and we answered, no, only Coke, she was not impressed and suspected we were under-age.

I noticed a lot of American soldiers sitting with their "Liebchens" but also older folks and many young people who were having a good time. The big band was very good; they played mostly Benny Goodman music (Muttchen called it outrageous) but we liked it very much. Twice our phone rang and Marleen answered. She was laughing and carried on a conversation I didn't really understand but I, too, had a good time and when a young man came and asked me if I would dance with him, I was very happy and forgot that time was flying and I had to go home soon to make it for my curfew.

Since we both danced very well, Marleen and I danced whenever we could and because it was more or less all American music, we learned quickly how to dance almost all of the dance steps that were in fashion after the war.

The young man I had already danced with came back but he seemed tipsy and started to come very close to me and I felt a bulge in his trousers. I tried hard to dance away from him, but he held tight and I was glad when the music stopped and he guided me back to our table. As soon he left, Marleen, who had just come back from the dance floor as well, laughed when I told her about it and said that she hadn't realized that I was so naïve but agreed that if I didn't like when he came too close, to push him away or tell him that I didn't want to dance right now and just leave.

I looked at my watch and saw that if I wanted to be home on time I had to leave at once. So I told Marleen that I had to go home right now and she answered that I was out of my mind because now it was just starting to be good.

"You can't go now because at about twelve o'clock the dancing waterfalls will start. This is the best thing you have ever seen, believe me, you can't miss that."

I wanted to stay, but on the other hand I knew Muttchen would be out of her mind and would think that something had happened to me. "No, I have to go home," I told Marleen, and she just shook her head and told me that I would have to go home by myself because she would not leave yet.

I could see she was upset, because she said, "I see it was a mistake to take you, and you are right, you should go home, after all you are not even sixteen."

I was mad at her for talking to me like that. She had known that I was almost two years younger than she was. And so I just said, "See you in school" and left.

I came home a bit late and Muttchen was already waiting for me. She was not pleased when she saw my make-up, which I had forgotten to wipe off before I came in, and told me, "So, not only are you late but look at you. Didn't I tell you that you were too young for make-up? And where were you?"

There was no way out, I had to tell her the truth, and she was shocked. But she didn't yell at me as I expected; she just told me that I mustn't go there anymore because I was too young. She paused for a while and then continued, "You will go to places like that when you are older, maybe more than I wish you to go, but not now. However, I am glad you told me the truth."

She carried on, "How did you get into the place? I understand they are very strict. Didn't you have to show your passport?" (After the war we had to have a passport at the age of fourteen.) I answered truthfully that Marleen knew somebody there and we had no problems getting in at all.

Muttchen was not impressed. She worried and even though she didn't show it, she was mad and said, "You mustn't see Marleen anymore."

But I answered, "She is a good friend and did nothing wrong. It was my fault. It will not happen again." She wouldn't give up but was more at ease when I told her that I only had one Coke. "Muttchen," I said, "it is so expensive there, but I would have liked to stay a bit longer to see the waterfalls. Apparently they are supposed to be so pretty and Marleen told me that many people just go there to see them play." By then she smiled and told me that maybe one day she would take me, but I only laughed and thought that she would run right back out if she heard the music.

Marleen still remained a good friend of mine, but she never asked me to go out with her again.

I told Reni about my new experience and right away she was all for going there too.

She said, "I tell you what, I will ask my father, and he will take us." (Reni's father, who had become blind after an accident, would do anything for his daughter.)

She made the arrangements and my Muttchen agreed that I could go with them.

It was just after my sixteenth birthday when her father took us and I felt so old and mature and happy that I could see the waterfalls dancing to the music.

Again, we had Coke and her father had a glass of wine. Our telephone rang quite often and most men called to ask why we were sitting with an old man. Some offered to help us and wanted to take us away, but we just laughed and stayed put. All we wanted was to see how the waterfalls danced. When the lights were turned down everybody clapped their hands and about thirty minutes later when the lights came on again everybody was delighted and gave a standing ovation. Reni's father wanted to know every detail and we explained to him the features and colours, and we saw from his facial expressions that he could "see" the picture.

After a while we had to go home and on the way out I saw Kurt. He must have seen me too because he came straight towards us.

Oh God, what does he want, what should I do, but there was not much time to think because in no time he was standing in front of us, stretching out his hand and saying, "Hello."

Reni's father asked us to whom we were talking but Kurt introduced himself to Reni's father as well. he explained that he was a customer of the sport store where

I worked. He smiled at me and said, "I am surprised to find you here."

But Reni mixed in and said, "I am one of Steffie's best friends and my father took us to see the waterfalls."

He looked surprised as if he expected something else so after a few more words we said our good-byes and as quickly as he came upon us, he disappeared again.

We waited for the streetcar and Reni whispered, "Kurt seems nice, but he looks like a professor. You didn't tell me that he wears glasses."

"So? But he is nice."

"I guess," Reni said.

But I noticed that she was not impressed. Maybe her doctor was a much better looking man, but was he as nice?

Kurt changed my life

It was spring when I saw Kurt again and when he invited me for dinner.

I found an excuse and told Muttchen that I was invited to eat at Reni's place, where they were celebrating her mother's birthday. My foster mother had no reason not to believe me because I was quite often at Reni's house.

However, I had to tell Reni about it as well so she wouldn't call on me while I was with Kurt.

Reni, my good friend, agreed at once to back me up and so, after I put on my new high heels and a fairly new dress, combed my hair ten times over and put some lipstick on, I left.

Kurt picked me up at the next street corner and we had dinner in a fine restaurant on Kurfuersten Damm, a very famous street in West Berlin.

While we had dinner, he couldn't take his eyes off me and I kind of felt uncomfortable and told him to stop looking at me. But instead of stopping he laughed and said, "You look much too pretty not to be looked at. Steffie, you have become a very beautiful young lady since I first met you, so let me admire you. Please!"

We had some wine with our dinner and I felt pretty

good, but after about two hours I told him that I had to go home because otherwise my foster mother would get suspicious. I told him about the lie and that I did not feel good about lying to my Muttchen. He agreed, but during our drive home he wanted to know why I lived with a foster mother and I explained to him that I loved my foster mother very much but did not get along with my birth mother.

"You must tell me the whole story one day. Let's say in two weeks?"

"In two weeks? What should I tell my foster mother? I can't lie again."

But he answered, "You will come up with something." From then on I started to lie a lot.

Reni helped me but warned me that I should be careful because if my mother ever found out about Kurt she would kill me.

Often I told Muttchen I was staying overnight with Reni so I could be out longer with Kurt. He had kissed me and I started to really like him. We talked about a lot of things and he must have realized that deep down I was very depressed and unsure of myself and now lying to my Muttchen didn't help.

One night he took me to a bar and I was drinking a bit more than usual. On our way out, when I thought we were going home, he stopped and told me he wanted to go to a hotel with me because he wanted us to be alone. Tipsy as I was I saw nothing wrong with that and agreed. He must have made arrangements prior to our arrival because he asked for the key as if he lived there.

Later, being alone with him, I became scared when we kissed again and he touched me in places where nobody had touched me before. But he didn't stop and ever so gently he undressed me and by that time I felt good and let him do what he wanted to do.

I was shocked about the pain and cried out but he took me in his arms and was gentle, and I became a woman.

When he brought me home he told me that he had to be careful because he was falling in love with me. And I too felt more and more that he was more to me than just a friend. Especially now after we had slept together.

At work I had to pretend that nothing had changed in my life because there, too, I lied about many things, but at home it was different altogether. Muttchen knew that something was different about me but she couldn't get a handle on it. She asked many questions, but I always had an answer. She even talked to Reni but Reni too lied for me.

When I was with Kurt, I was happy and thought I was free from all the weight I had had to carry. But deep down, I was very unhappy. I knew he was too old for me; we were twenty-two years apart in age and Muttchen would have a fit if I ever brought him home.

At school I skipped and missed many classes, so that my employer even received a letter. He questioned me about what was going on and again I had an answer and lied myself out of it and he was satisfied, but warned me to catch up and get on top of things again because he didn't want me to fail.

His wife still brought their son over for baby-sitting but now I was scared to tell them that I didn't like doing it and that it didn't fit into my job description.

Yes, I realized Kurt had changed my life.

The break-up

ONE DAY I WAS SO UNHAPPY ABOUT IT ALL, I WANTED TO TELL him that we had to stop seeing each other. I talked to him about it but he wouldn't accept it. He looked at me and said, "Don't do this to me, because I have fallen in love with you." Since I thought I loved him too I couldn't bring myself to tell him to leave me alone and that it was over. It would have been the best for us, but it didn't happen.

It was fall by now and Muttchen planned a trip to her relatives in Magdeburg. She told me she would stay for a week and that she trusted me to stay alone with Frau Moritz, our tenant. I told her not to worry and to have a good time.

I told Kurt about Muttchen's plans and he smiled and said that he, too, had plans to go on a trip, but on business, and could I arrange to come with him. I thought about it and since I had some holidays coming, I agreed.

Muttchen left early in the morning and after she was gone I informed Frau Moritz that I would stay with Reni.

Kurt and I left later, after I finished work and had my hair done.

The first three days were wonderful; beside his visits with customers we did some sight- seeing and we had a lot of fun. And, of course, we would go out and would make love. Everything was so new for me. We told each other that we were totally in love and I thought he would propose to me and we would get engaged. But I was so wrong because I was so naïve.

Two days before we were to return home, Kurt was told to return a phone call he had received while we were out. He went down to make the call since there were no phones in the hotel rooms and when he came back his face was as white as chalk. I looked at him and knew something was drastically wrong. However, what he told me took my breath away. He said, "My wife knows about us. I am in big trouble."

At first I didn't understand and I said, "Your wife? You're married?"

He answered, "I always wanted to tell you, but we were so happy that I didn't have the nerve to tell the truth." He came towards me.

I didn't know what to say and started to cry. And when he came and wanted to comfort me, I pushed him away and screamed, "Don't touch me! DON'T!!"

"Steffie, don't push me away, I love you! I told my wife long before we went on this trip that I wanted a divorce. We had problems before you and I met. She suspected that I was having an affair when I told her I wanted a divorce. So now she told me that she has known about us for a long time because she had a detective on me. She wanted to have proof that I was the guilty one, so that she would receive everything we owned, including custody of our little girl.

I looked at him even more disgusted than before.

"You have a child as well? You pig, you!"

He answered, "Yes, I am sorry, I didn't think things over. I am so sorry because I don't know what I would do without you. But you have to understand, we have to part, at least for now."

I looked at him and I realized at that moment that I was no better than my mother was. She got involved with a married man as well. He had children and now I hoped that I was not pregnant, because that would complete the picture.

I suddenly wanted to run. I wanted to go to my Muttchen. And I became so sad because I realized that I told her all those lies. Would she ever forgive me? And my mother? What would she do to me if she heard what I had done? Oh God, I prayed, forgive me. Help me!

We left an hour after he called his home. I was too stunned to say a word or even cry. I felt cold, so very cold. We stopped once because I had to go to the bathroom. He drove like a maniac, but I didn't care, I was just trying to find a way of telling my Muttchen what had happened. Would she understand? She would come back in two days; by then I would have to think of a way of telling her without hurting her. How, I didn't know.

We arrived early in the morning in Berlin and Kurt stopped in front of our apartment building. Just before we arrived he told me that he practically lived around the corner, about two blocks away from us. I just looked at him. I couldn't understand. I was empty.

When I got out of the car, he told me I would hear from him, but I said, "Don't bother. Don't ever come near me again."

As soon he was out of my sight I started to cry. I rang the bell because I had forgotten my keys. At first I had a hard time finding the right bell knob because my tears were blinding me but I found it. I waited to hear the buzzer and I needed a handkerchief but had none. It started to rain and my hair was hanging down and still the buzzer didn't hum. Was Frau Moritz not home? Oh God, help me, I needed to get in. I needed to think clearly. I was so very tired and I wanted to sleep. Just when I was about to give up, the buzzer hummed and I was able to open the door.

Frau Moritz stood at the door, surprised when she saw me, and said, "Steffie, I was sleeping. I expected you tomorrow. Didn't you like it at your girlfriend's?"

I was tempted to say that I wasn't with Reni, that I had lied, that I was like my mother, a bad person, but I said nothing. I just hoped that she didn't notice that I was crying.

I lifted my little suitcase and took the five steps up to our apartment and still didn't answer. I slipped by her and went into our room. I heard her say that if I needed her, I should call her, and then she went into her room. I heard her door close.

It was all quiet now and I sat down. My tears came back and I couldn't stop crying. My mother came into my head and I heard her screaming, "You whore, you! How low can you get!" And in my mind I saw her lifting her hand to strike me as she always did when she thought I had done something wrong.

I saw my Muttchen, her eyes so sad and disappointed. I heard her say, "Why did you lie? You should have told me. We would have found a way to get out of this without so much hurt. Oh Steffchen, you always know that you can talk to me. Why didn't you come to me?" I saw her taking me in her arms, as she always did when I was in need of feeling her love. I needed her closeness, but she was not there. I was alone and suddenly I wanted to sleep, I wanted to die! Because I was like my mother, I was bad and had no reason to criticize her anymore. I was like her.

I went to my bed and lay down. I took my doll in my arm and wanted to sleep. I was so scared of my mother now that I wanted to vomit and then I knew what I had to do. I got up, took my keys, and went to a drugstore near by. I bought a pack of fifteen sleeping pills. I chose a small quantity, since I didn't want to risk being questioned for whom these pills were. And then I walked on to another drugstore and bought another fifteen pills. Would it be enough? I didn't know so I bought another package and had three little bottles with fifteen tablets in each. I was sure now that these little pills would give me the sleep I needed to stop thinking about what my mother would do to me if she heard what I had done.

I became very calm now, no more tears, no more fear. I looked at the pills and I was relieved, because pretty soon I would sleep. I just hoped that God would understand and would forgive me, because I knew that what I was planning was not right. But I had no other choice. I was like my mother, and she was right, I was a whore.

I had to go pee first and realized that I was not pregnant. I had started my period. So at least that was OK.

I went to the kitchen to get a glass of water. Frau Moritz was making lunch and she asked me if I wanted something but of course I was not hungry, I just wanted to sleep. She must have noticed that I was not myself and asked if I was not feeling well but I said I had a headache. She accepted that answer because she knew that I had had migraine headaches since I was thirteen.

I took a large glass of water and went back to my room. It was not enough and repeatedly I got glasses of water from the kitchen and Frau Moritz asked again if I was OK. I told her that I was very thirsty.

By now I had swallowed about three-quarters of the tablets I bought. I started to get dizzy and wanted to lie down. I took my doll again and must have gone towards my bed but I'm not sure if I made it.

I heard my mother yelling, "You whore, you!" and saw her laughing and saying, "And you wanted to be better than me!" And then I heard my foster mother saying, "Rosi, leave her alone, can't you see she is upset?" Again, my mother didn't stop, wanting to hit me, but my foster mother stopped her and I ran away and came to a meadow full of yellow flowers. It was so pretty! When I looked further I saw a bright light that shone down on me. It seemed like a road sign. I wanted to go there to see where it would take me. I turned around and saw Muttchen waving and calling me, "Steffchen come back." But I didn't want to come back, because I knew my mother would hit me, so I ran further. I waved back and told my Muttchen not to be sad. I saw her crying, waving and saying "Come back," but then I did not want to turn around again.

Where was I?

AND THEN I FELT AS IF SOMEBODY SHOOK ME AND SAID, "WAKE up!!!!" But I didn't want to wake up. I looked at the flowers and ran even further. It was quiet again but then that somebody who shook me before didn't seem to stop, didn't give up, and I had no other choice. I woke up. I saw people looking down on me and somebody said, "We have her back!"

Where was I? I wanted to go back where I saw the pretty flowers. But instead I saw people with white coats and nurses? Was I in a hospital? I woke up.

A man in a white coat bent over me and said with a friendly smile, "Here you are, it's about time, we almost lost you. Why did you do it?" And I thought, do what? I didn't know what he was talking about. I felt sick to my stomach and wanted to throw up. I lifted my head but fell back and the person who talked to me before told somebody to call for a bed, and then I must have fallen asleep again, because when I woke up the next time, I saw my mother.

She didn't hit me, she didn't look furious, but she didn't say anything either. She just looked at me without emotion, not sad, not happy, nothing.

The doctor came in and looked down on me. He stroked my hair and asked, "How are we doing?" I didn't answer. My mother answered for me, "I think she is fine. How long will she have to stay here?" I moved my head and asked if my Muttchen was here, if she knew. The doctor turned to my mother and asked her who Muttchen was and my mother explained.

I ignored my mother and said to the doctor, "I want to talk to my foster mother. I want to go home to her, not to my mother's."

The doctor took my mother to the side and they had a discussion and after quite a long time the nice doctor came back and explained that my foster mother was not home yet and when she did come back I would be released to go home to her. He told me not to worry. He would look after me. I fell asleep again and must have slept for a long time because when I woke up I was on intravenous and a nurse was watching me.

A day later I felt better and was transferred to another room with many beds.

My mother came again, but I didn't want to talk to her, and after a while she told me that she knew all of the details and I should be ashamed of myself. Then she left.

After a week I was released to go home to my Muttchen. I still can't remember how I got home. Did she pick me up? Did my mother? It's all a blank.

My mother came to see us a few days later and wanted me to sign some papers. Apparently she wanted to sue Kurt for getting involved with a minor. I told her I would not sign the document because it was my fault as well. And I said that I would not go back to work. "I can't!"

We had an argument and my foster mother stepped in and said, "Enough!"

"Rosi, I think she is right, if you go to court she has to go through the agony again. She would have to explain all of the details and this would be too much for her. She already feels guilty. Yes, she is just sixteen and he should have known better, but let it be."

My mother argued that he should pay for what he did, but Muttchen answered, "Rosi, let it be! As you know, we have an appointment with her guardian and I am sure he will suggest what should be done. Give her time, the wounds will heal and then we will see further."

My mother was livid now, but my Muttchen stayed calm and told her that everything would be fine.

"As you know, Rosi, we all made our mistakes. At least we should be happy that she is not pregnant."

My mother left shortly afterwards, without even saying good-bye, but I was glad that she was gone.

I cried a lot or just sat there without saying a word. At night I was scared to go to sleep because I was having nightmares. I was depressed, had claustrophobia, and at times was not able to breathe properly. I was a mess. And on top of all of that, my headaches became worse.

Muttchen talked to me often about my ordeal and told me to just try to think about it as a bad experience.

"Just be careful the next time. Although you will think differently, there will be another one. Just make sure that you don't get hurt again. Talk to me; at least I can give you some advice." And then she told me her story, the misery she had had to go through.

A few days later we saw my guardian. My mother and Willi came too.

We were invited to come into the office; however, when my mother was asked who Willi was and explained, he was asked to wait outside.

In a short summary I had to tell my guardian what had happened and was asked if we planned to sue. Muttchen and I said no, my mother said yes, and it was concluded not to sue because as my guardian explained, it would not be wise since we had both been willing to go into the relationship. He also pointed out that Kurt's wife could sue me for adultery and the consequences wouldn't be pretty. So it was best to keep it as it was.

We had to go to court anyway because I wanted to dissolve the contract I had with my employer. It was a short but eye-opening experience, because it taught me not to take a signed contract as a joke. As a matter of fact it is a very serious matter, I was told. The judge explained to me that there were almost always consequences to pay. "So the next time you go to sign something, make sure you can hold up your part of the agreement before you actually sign it."

And a month later I was without work and not in school. I had missed one year of school now, which would still give me a chance to become something more than a cleaning woman. But because of all the misery I had gone through lately, I was lost and didn't know how to continue.

I didn't see Kurt for the longest time and when I saw him from a far distance again I felt disgusted with myself for ever having fallen in love with this man. Had it been love? The attraction, whatever it was, was gone. He had walked into my life and, after much damage, had walked right back out again. He had changed my life all right but when I look back now, maybe for the better. He made me grow up very fast, as if I hadn't already grown up too quickly already because of the war and all the other circumstances at the time. But I guess such is life.

I learned that Frau Moritz had saved my life and that Reni went to Kurt and his wife and gave them a piece of her mind by telling them as it was, that Kurt should have acted as a responsible adult and not taken advantage of me. And that his wife shouldn't have any ideas about suing me for breaking up her marriage because he had known how young I was.

Reni tried to help me to forget the past and to look forward to the future. She was a good friend. However, shortly after my dilemma, I broke up with all my friends including Marleen. I was ashamed of myself and had to take some distance from all of the people who knew about my big mistake.

I am turning my life around

MUTTCHEN BECAME UPSET WITH ME BECAUSE I LOST MY SPUNK. The only thing I still did was to go to my swim club, but all my other interests were gone. I stopped laughing and in some ways, living. I lost a lot of weight because I hardly ever ate.

Muttchen complained that I wasn't working or finishing school. She would say, "Steffchen, what will become out of you?"

And I would look at her and would answer straight-faced, "Something I guess, maybe a whore, that's what my mother calls me anyway."

And she would get so mad at me. One day she almost lost her temper and her last words came out screaming: "Do something with your life, you are so smart, the world is all open to you, just do something and grab it. I cannot stand by and see you waste your talents. Wake up. You did wrong but you can do right again."

I saw tears in her eyes, tears that were usually never visible. It ripped my heart out and I guess it made me think. She was right! She was telling me the truth! I must do something to get out of this rut.

I started to read the newspapers again and listened

to music. I was still in another world at times, still had claustrophobia and nightmares and still felt unclean when I thought how right my mother was, but for the first time I felt that I was on the mend and wanted to show her that I was not like her after all. It was my intention to make my Muttchen proud and show my mother that she was wrong about me.

Shortly after I changed my attitude about myself, I started looking at advertisements and found an interesting one: Memmert, Private Business College, one- and two-year courses to start in October 1953.

I looked carefully at the advertisement and found that this would give me the opportunity to get my education and maybe a job I could be proud of.

I showed Muttchen the ad and after she too read it carefully she shook her head, "This sounds good but where should I take the money from? As you can see, this is a private institution."

I was upset but I understood what she was talking about. I looked at her for a while and then had a brainstorm. "Maybe Children's Aid, my guardian, could help. Could we not ask him?"

She smiled, and answered, "So I see your brain is working again."

We both laughed and then I said, "Seriously Muttchen, don't you think we could?"

"It's worth a try," she answered, "but don't you think you should first call this school and ask for details so we have facts when we go and ask for help from the government?"

I agreed and the next morning I went to a close-by phone booth and called. I spoke to a nice female voice and told her of my interest in attending the college and she connected me to a Professor Dr. Memmert, obviously the director of the school. He too was very nice and asked me to come for an interview. And so the next day I went for the interview. It took almost one and a half hours by train to get there and I just thought about the fare and the books, etc., and almost gave up my hopes of attending the school before I even talked to him.

The school was located in a very big private villa, very close to the train station, for which I was thankful. My heart almost came out of my throat when I entered the building.

I was asked to wait outside the office and for a while I wanted to leave before the interview took place but then I thought that I mustn't give up. Maybe this was my chance. I told myself, "You must stay, don't run away."

I didn't have to wait too long and was called into a simple little office. A tall young woman smiled at me and said, "The professor will be with you shortly." And a bit later the door to another office opened and a tiny man with white hair and very sharp, strict eyes came towards me and asked if I was Steffie, and when I just moved my head because my voice had left me, he waved me into his office. He introduced himself as Dr. Memmert and extended his hand to say hello.

I couldn't believe that he was the owner/director of this school. Or was it just a joke? Except for his eyes, he looked more like a dwarf than a professor.

Anyway, he signaled me to sit down and then walked behind a fairly big desk and sat down too, his eyes never leaving mine. The office was a bit bigger than the one belonging to his secretary. It was very tidy, with many bookshelves filled with books and files. Some files were scattered on his desk and he quickly piled them up to a stack. He looked very busy.

At first he said nothing and kept looking at me and I felt uncomfortable, but then he finally started to talk and explained the courses this institute had to offer. He came quickly to the point and I had to tell him what I wanted to be and how I saw my future. He asked for my report cards. Thank heavens I had them with me and was able to show them to him and after he glanced at them he said he would be willing to take me on. But then he spoke about the tuition fee and I stood up and apologized for wasting his time because, I explained, my foster mother would not be able to pay that kind of money. He didn't seem to be surprised about the money situation and asked, "Your foster mother?"

"Yes, I am a foster child and we are poor. The only thing that would make it possible is if my guardian would be able to help, but I doubt it, it is simply too much money."

His strict eyes became softer and he answered that he might be able to help if I would be willing to do the course in half the time. I looked up and asked, "Is that possible?"

"Yes, it is, but it would take a lot of willpower and a lot of work. Also, I suggest that you talk to your guardian. I am sure that you would be more successful in explaining what we need to do. Your report cards are good and with this course you would be able to complete your high school and would receive your business diploma as well. But I warn you, you will have to work your buns off. I don't offer what I am offering you very often. As a matter of fact you are the first, but I like you and I think we can do it."

"One more thing before we go on, explain to me why you broke your contract as an apprentice in the sport store?"

I was quiet for a moment and then I said, "I realized that that was not what I wanted to be, a sales clerk. I need something that keeps me more interested."

He smiled saying, "That is understandable. I just hope that office work will capture your interest." A quiet moment again, and then, "Do you have the phone number of your guardian?"

I was proud to have the number handy and answered, "Yes, I do," and gave it to him.

"I will call him, and you call me back in about three days."

I was speechless and didn't know how to take everything in. After taking a long deep breath I agreed to call him back.

I was still worried about the money my Muttchen had to come up with and thought about the cost of the fare for the train, etc., but then I hoped that we would manage somehow.

Before I left, he showed me the classrooms and I realized it was a small institution but, with it being only eight years after the war, it seemed sufficiently equipped with typewriters and whatever was needed for a college and I swore to myself that I would do my best to graduate with good marks, if my guardian would provide the funds.

When I returned home I was so excited that I was hardly able to explain to my Muttchen what had happened and how the interview went. When I finally finished, I realized that she was a bit skeptical but in principle I think she believed in me like always.

The next day the lady from the corner store came

rushing over and told Muttchen to call my guardian. A long time ago she had agreed that we could give him her business number since we had no phone.

Anyway, Muttchen returned his call right away and we had to see him the following day. We were both very excited and I prayed that I could enroll in the college. When we stepped into his office I saw his smile and I knew something good was going to happen. His first words were, "I am proud of you, Steffie. I guess you are going to college."

Muttchen interrupted and asked right away, "How much do I have to pay because you know I have almost no income."

And again he smiled and said, "The government will pay the tuition if you agree to waive the monthly child support for the duration of the course, which I understand will be six months because Steffie is agreeing to finish the course in half the usual time."

"Also you will get support for books and we will reimburse the fare for the train. After she completes the course, Professor Memmert has agreed to provide her with a job should she be able to complete every subject above average."

Muttchen and I looked at each other, and I said, "And if I fail?"

"You won't! I know that because I know you; you will not let this go by because you will not pass up a chance of a lifetime."

Muttchen smiled, "I am surprised that you too learned to know her that well, because many people don't know my Steffchen, that if she wants something, she does what she has to do to go after it."

The next morning I called Dr. Memmert and said, "I guess you know already, but I could start on October 1st."

And he answered, "I am looking forward to seeing you in class."

The way to happiness

WE WERE ABOUT TWELVE GIRLS AND THREE BOYS IN MY CLASS. My main subjects were accounting, shorthand, typing, business, and administration.

Since I took a double course I had to study double the amount and at first I thought I would never accomplish what I had promised. I hated shorthand and typing. I loved accounting and business and administration.

After about three weeks I knew I would never be great in the two subjects I hated and I went to Dr. Memmert and told him about my dilemma. He agreed because he had noticed already and told me that I must do my best but should concentrate on the subjects I loved. He would help so I would be able to continue with all the subjects. But he repeated, "Concentrate on accounting and business and administration." He smiled, saying, "Not everybody will become a secretary."

I did just that and had no problems with the pace required to get through the courses to accomplish what I had in mind.

At first I had absolutely no interest in looking at my classmates. I found them all a bit stuck-up and felt that I didn't belong there. A bit later some of the girls started to talk to me during breaks and I actually found them to be pleasant and even helpful.

I still had bad dreams about the war and Poland, and my mother calling me bad names. Sometimes I dreamt that I was running naked with an airplane flying above me and when I looked up I saw the bombs coming down. I would run and run until I woke up, screaming and soaked from sweat. Or my mother would come towards me, laughing and saying repeatedly, "You whore. You whore."

Muttchen wanted me to see a doctor about it, but I refused, because I didn't want to be branded as mental, which is what we called people with some of the problems I had.

I started to have anxiety attacks and didn't want to go to see a movie unless I had an aisle seat. But I had no problems when I was in school. I loved it and I was truly happy to be there. And now that I was pretty much accepted by many of my classmates, I was even more comfortable. I was not the outsider anymore and felt as if I belonged.

I saw my mother very seldom but missed my little brother. He was five by now and a big boy. When I saw him we still had that closeness with each other and he would run towards me and would give me a big kiss. We truly loved each other. I am sure that if I would have had a closer relationship with my mother and Willi I would have seen him a lot, but as it was I didn't see much of him.

I guess it was in November when one of the boys in school came to class completely drunk. He hardly made it into the classroom, sat on his stool, and during class slipped down to the floor and slept. Everybody kind of laughed but didn't let on and didn't give it away so that

Dr. Memmert, who taught that morning, wouldn't notice. During lunch the other boys dragged him up and we went outside, where he waved a banana in front of a policeman's face and almost got arrested.

Anyway, during all that commotion he always looked at me and had this funny grin on his face. One girl said to me, "I think he has a crush on you."

I looked at her and said, "No, he's just drunk and doesn't even know whom he is smiling at."

"No, really," she shook her head. "He looks at you all the time, not only now. Did you never notice?"

"No, I never noticed, and I am not really interested either."

"You're not? He is the best-looking guy around here that I can think of, and you say you are not interested?"

"No," I said. "I am not!"

The next day he came in sober and somewhat embarrassed. I watched him and noticed that he really had his eyes on me. I pretended not to notice. Yes, he was good looking, tall, with broad shoulders and had almost black hair like I had. But surely he was too young for me. And why me? I looked around. The other girls looked so much prettier, so, why me?

Shortly after that he started to talk to me, asking me where I lived and so on. He then noticed that I had quite a way to come to school and told me where he came from and that he often took his bike.

I realized that he lived in a very expensive neighbourhood and he must have noticed that where I came from was not the best area in Berlin. Shortly afterwards when we had to go back to class, I made sure to keep my distance from him.

For a few days we hardly spoke and I was glad, but at times I caught myself thinking about him. I told myself that I mustn't do that because we came from different worlds and somehow I started to develop a complex about it.

When we were on break, I stayed with the girls but they started to talk constantly about the three boys. Most of them talked about Dietmar and how they noticed that he had his eyes on me. I, of course, denied it and told them it was all in their minds, but at the same time I was flattered. I started to think about him more often than I wanted.

Just before our short Christmas break he came to me and wished me a great Christmas and a happy New Year and in his eyes I could read that he was sorry that we couldn't celebrate together. And honestly, I was sorry too, but didn't show my thoughts and just wished him good holidays as well.

We returned to college shortly after the new year and the work I had was brutal now but I didn't let this slow me down. I kept up with the work and didn't think about anything else except suddenly Dietmar sneaked more into my head than I wanted. I couldn't get him out of my mind. I sure didn't need that or him at all.

One day we had a lot of snow during the night and the next morning, getting to college was quite a challenge. Many made it and classes were not cancelled as some had hoped.

During the lunch break many stayed in but some of us wanted fresh air and we went out for a walk. Of course the snow was inviting and the boys started a snowball fight.

I was worried that my hair would be messed-up and

ran away from the group, when I noticed Dietmar was close behind me. What to do? I just stopped running and turned and said. "Don't!" But he was now so close behind me that I actually could feel the snow in my face. He looked in my eyes and dropped the snowball and said, "Would you like to go out with me, let's say on Saturday? We could go and see a movie or have something to eat."

I must have been so surprised because this was the last thing I had expected. "You mean a date? You want to take me out on a date?"

"Yes, a date! Would you come?" His brown eyes were so full of honesty and hope that I was moved and said, "Where would we meet, where would you take me?"

"Oh, I could pick you up from close to where you live, maybe at the train station? And from there we could go back by train to Kurfuersten Damm or something."

And just for a moment I thought, here you go again Steffie, and then I said, "All right, Saturday at six at Neukoelln train station. Don't come out, because you will have to pay the fare again. I will meet you inside instead."

He smiled and said, "I have a card, good for the month, don't you?"

And I laughed and answered, "I didn't think about the card, I just wanted to save you some money."

True love

WE WERE BOTH ON TIME AND HAD A GOOD TIME TOGETHER. I learned that he came from a very well-off family but had both feet on the ground. I discovered later that he took all his savings to make this date work.

After the movie he brought me home and we kissed and I realized that this was so different and honest, and it was very tempting to fall in love.

He had to rush back to the station—otherwise he would have missed the last train—and so we did not have much time to say good-bye, but we were both shocked about our feelings. After all, we had never talked much in college. So what happened to us?

On Monday we didn't know how to behave. He waved shyly and I smiled back but we didn't talk until lunch break. And even then we didn't say much because, as he told me later, we were both afraid that one of us would end the short relationship.

He mentioned that he missed the second train when he had to transfer and was in trouble at home because he missed his curfew.

I told him I was in trouble too, because I was home too late also, since my Muttchen didn't know that we were actually just outside in the doorway. Of course I didn't tell her that and so she was worried I was going to be in trouble again.

I told her before I went out that I had a date with a classmate and that we wanted to go to Kurfuersten Damm to see a movie but she still worried, which I understood. Also, when I told her where he lived, she said right away, "Steffie, he is not suitable to go out with."

I looked at her and took her in my arms. "You always see the worst, Muttchen, I am not going to marry him, we just want to see a movie together, so please don't worry."

During the week we hardly had time to talk. I had so much work now that all I could think about was to finish the course successfully.

But on Saturdays Dietmar and I would meet and sometimes just go for walks. I was trying to keep this just as a friendship. Sure we kissed, but that was it. But I was scared.

Dietmar knew that I would finish the course earlier than the rest of the class. He mentioned that he hoped that we would continue seeing each other and that he was worried that we would part and I would have other interests. I looked at him and told him what my Muttchen said regarding the different backgrounds we came from. "This," I said, "will always keep us apart whether we want it to or not. So, it would be better to part now rather than later."

"Steffie," he looked at me with his big eyes, "how could you say that? What have my parents to do with us? Don't you know that I have fallen in love with you?"

"You can't say that, Dietmar, we have just gone out a few times. You will change your mind when you don't see me every day anymore, just you wait and see."

"I won't change my mind. I fell in love with you when

I saw you the first time, so don't talk to me about my love for you."

"We will see," I answered. And we left it at that.

In mid-March I was called into the office. I was scared that Dr. Memmert would tell me that I was not doing too well because my shorthand was terrible. However, the typing wasn't bad and my tests in accounting and administration always came back with very high marks. Still, I was not too sure of the outcome.

When Dr. Memmert came toward me I realized that something good was to happen. He had a big smile on his face, and when he told me to sit down and went around to sit behind his desk, as he did when we met the first time, I knew this meeting would turn out to be a positive one.

Again he looked at me for a long time and finally said, "I have scheduled an interview for you. The interview is with a large well-known cleaner and laundry company, located in Berlin-Britz. The company is about an hour from where you live but with a streetcar stop right in the front of the door. These people are interested in somebody who is very good in accounting and customer relations, and I think you are qualified and good in both. The salary at first will not be great because they intend to train you further for approximately six months and by the time you are finished, you would be able to work in almost all departments in their office. Your salary would go up accordingly. The company employs two hundred people in their plant and approximately thirty people in the office plus eighty-five people in their stores. This company would give you the opportunity you deserve, Steffie. It's a good deal."

He gave me the full address and directions on how to

get there, and the next day, April 1, 1954, I was employed and started my new job.

I was so scared when I went for the interview but when I heard that I had the job, I could have hugged the world.

Muttchen had tears in her eyes and we both danced around, not letting go of each other. We were both so happy and proud that we had done it. Because, after all, I never would have been able to do it without her help and support.

Dietmar was also happy for me but he was sad that I was leaving school earlier than he was, and said, "It will not be the same without you. But we will see each other again, right?"

And I took him in my arms and said, "Yes, we will see each other again, I am almost sure of it."

I truly enjoyed my new job and was always sad when I had to change departments, but it gave me the opportunity to gain insight into more than one job, and gave me the opportunity to learn how business is done.

My first paycheque was not much but I was proud of myself and was kind of shocked when Muttchen made a rule that I had to give her ten percent of my pay for, as she called it, room and board. (I learned later that she didn't spend one penny of it but saved it until I got married.)

After Dietmar finished school he took on an apprenticeship as a textile mechanic.

The idea was that Dietmar would later work in his father's business, a textile wholesale company. He did work for his father, for maybe six weeks, but then had to quit because they couldn't get along.

When my Muttchen met Dietmar the first time, she told me as soon as he left that he was much too young for me and I should end the relationship at once. And she added, "You will see that you simply don't fit into his family."

I argued that, of course, and in time she accepted him and did so with all her heart. He became her darling "Dietmar" who could do no wrong.

And when I met Dietmar's parents I realized that Muttchen was right, I didn't belong there and his parents let me know it and made me feel it whenever there was an opportunity. But Dietmar stayed by my side and on April 6, 1957, we were married.

Not far from Muttchen's place we rented a cute room. In 1957 apartments were not yet in the cards and we were sure that we didn't want to live with his parents, or even with my Muttchen. I just wanted to be with my Dietmar. Alone, on our own!

Muttchen gave us money for either a wedding party or for furniture. We chose the furniture and paid for a small but nice party ourselves. And later, when Dietmar took me in his arms and carried me over the threshold of our little one-room paradise, we were both in a world of happiness I never ever thought I would experience.

Epilogue

WHEN DIETMAR AND I CELEBRATED OUR FIFTIETH ANNIVER-
sary, Dean, our son, presented a PowerPoint DVD show
to our guests. He showed pictures of us going back as far
as our childhood as well as pictures of the fifty years of
our life together, our children, grandchildren, our family
still in Berlin, and friends here in Canada. So many memories, nicely sorted, with music and laughter and tears.

When we left Germany, with our little three-year-old
daughter Sabrina and three suitcases, in December 1961
to immigrate to Canada, we had no idea of the future
ahead of us and where it would bring us. We arrived at
Toronto Airport and we were full of hope.

Our family and friends didn't understand why we
wanted to leave Berlin. But we made the decision to leave
because Dietmar and I didn't want to raise our daughter
with a "wall" all around us.

The East German government, supported by Russia,
built that wall more or less overnight on August 13, 1961,
to separate the East from the West completely. Too many
people had packed up their belongings to work and live in
the West and so they had to do something about it. The
wall lasted 28 years and came down in November 1989.

The day after our fiftieth wedding anniversary we sat in our kitchen and over a cup of coffee started to reminisce about the many years we had now spent in Canada. We talked about the hardship and the joy we had experienced and how quickly the years had gone by, how many friends we now had and how our family had grown.

At the party we were surrounded by all our friends, our children and four grandchildren, two boys from our daughter and two boys from our son.

Dean and Denise, our daughter-in-law, made it a truly wonderful celebration. The pictures showed how far the time together had brought us.

And then the big surprise: Dietmar's cousin came from Germany to celebrate with us. He was with us for only three days but what a wonderful feeling it gave us because he was with us at our wedding as well.

Our walk down memory lane was endless, and again and again our memories went back to our loved ones, as sadly, many are not with us anymore. We certainly laughed about the fact that Dietmar's parents had only given our marriage about a year to last!

LaVergne, TN USA
10 September 2010
196631LV00003B/7/P